Preventing Occupational Exposures to Infectious Disease in Health Care

Amber Hogan Mitchell

Preventing Occupational Exposures to Infectious Disease in Health Care

A Practical Guide

 Springer

Amber Hogan Mitchell
International Safety Center, Inc.
League City, TX
USA

University of Maryland School of Medicine
Division of Occupational and
Environmental Medicine
Baltimore, MD
USA

ISBN 978-3-030-56041-6   ISBN 978-3-030-56039-3   (eBook)
https://doi.org/10.1007/978-3-030-56039-3

This Springer imprint is published by the registered company Springer Nature Switzerland AG
The registered company address is: Gewerbestrasse 11, 6330 Cham, Switzerland

In memory of:

My mom – Jane Culwell Hogan

My stepmom – Patricia Kolmer

My gram – Eugenia "Jean" Warfield Culwell

This is in honor of them, and to current and future generations of healthcare heroes serving others in every corner of the globe.

The world would not turn without you.

Foreword

Hospitals are dangerous places to work—injury and illness rates among healthcare workers is far higher than the rates among construction workers or coal miners. Keeping healthcare workers safe is the key to keeping patients safe. An important component of this is prevention of infectious disease.

If anyone doubted the importance of preventing occupational exposure to infectious disease in healthcare settings, the global COVID-19 pandemic surely changed that. Healthcare workers were on the front line, fighting the epidemic and saving lives. Thousands of these workers were sickened by the virus, and many died.

Failure to adequately protect healthcare workers contributed to the spread of the epidemic. The absence of adequate preventive programs, especially at the beginning of the epidemic, infected some workers and required many to be quarantined. This left fewer to treat patients, making the work of the remaining workers that much more difficult and increasing their risk of infection.

Protecting healthcare workers from infectious disease is not rocket science. We know how to do it right, enabling healthcare workers to be safe while providing the best care to patients and clients.

Much of what needs to be done is explained in clear terms in this book, *Preventing Occupational Exposures to Infectious Disease in Health Care: A Practical Guide*. Dr. Amber Hogan Mitchell uses her decades of experience in occupational safety and health and infection prevention to provide valuable information and practical guidance that will be useful to anyone in the healthcare sector.

David Michaels, PhD, MPH
Professor of Environmental and Occupational Health
Milken Institute School of Public Health
The George Washington University
Washington, DC, USA

Former Assistant Secretary of Labor for the
Occupational Safety and Health
Administration (2009–2017)

Acknowledgments

This book is a labor of love. It is the culmination of years of learning from the tireless work of my mentors, teachers, colleagues, friends, and family. It is because of the instillation of their dedication and humility in so many of us that it was necessary to write it all down so that it could serve others. My grandfather was the first physician I knew, and his running off with medical bag in hand to deliver babies and provide medical care at all hours of the day and night imprinted in me the desire to serve professionals like him.

Thank you to those that have influenced my life and career: GWU, Binghamton, USUHS, the US Army, Indian Health Service, Public Health Service, Faccia Luna, OSHA, NIOSH, CDC, BD, University of Texas, J&J, Vestagen, International Safety Center, APHA OHS Section, NIEHS, University of Maryland, and each and every healthcare worker I have had the honor to know and work with.

E pluribus unum.

Many images in this book were created by Chelsey Armstrong, an exceptionally talented artist and graphic designer. Thank you Chelsey for sharing your gifts for the benefit of public health.

Thank you to Springer Senior Editor Janet Kim, who graciously guided me through this writing, editing, and publication process. You made something this daunting manageable and enjoyable.

Gratitude to Heather Monaghan, whose idea this was in the first place. Thank you!

Thank you to my husband—John Christopher Mitchell. Every human deserves a cheerleader as true as you. You make me laugh and keep me strong.

Contents

About the Author

Amber Hogan Mitchell, DrPH, MPH, CPH, is currently the International Safety Center's President and Executive Director. The Center distributes the Exposure Prevention Information Network (or "EPINet") free to hospitals to measure occupational exposures to blood and body fluid and other potentially infectious materials that cause illness and infection in the working population. EPINet is the world's most widely used surveillance tool for this type of data and has been distributed to thousands of US hospitals and nearly 100 countries.

Dr. Mitchell's career has been focused on public health and occupational safety and health related to infectious disease. She has worked in the public, private, and academic sectors. Dr. Mitchell began her career as the very first OSHA National Bloodborne Pathogens Coordinator and a Senior Industrial Hygienist and has received several Secretary of Labor Excellence awards for her work on healthcare worker safety as well as bioterrorism and public preparedness. She sat on a team of dedicated professionals that integrated the Needlestick Safety and Prevention Act into the regulatory landscape.

Dr. Mitchell has held regulatory and medical affairs positions for medical device companies. As a doctoral scholar with Centers for Disease Control and Prevention (CDC) and National Institute for Occupational Safety and Health (NIOSH), she completed her Doctor of Public Health (DrPH) degree at the University of Texas School of Public Health. She holds a Bachelor's Degree in Psychology from Binghamton University and a Master's Degree in Public Health from The George Washington University. Dr. Mitchell is Certified in Public Health as an esteemed member of the very first CPH cohort offered by the National Board of Public Health Examiners. She was the 2019 Chair of the Occupational Health and Safety (OHS) Section of the American Public Health Association (APHA).

Dr. Mitchell continues to serve the country as a senior science advisor for the National Institute of Environmental Health Sciences (NIEHS) for Worker Training Program for COVID-19. She is also Adjunct Faculty at the University of Maryland School of Medicine, Department of Occupational and Environmental Medicine.

She will continue to fight for a world where there is no illness or infection as a result of one's work.

Dr. Mitchell also has a passion for nutrition, dietetics, and wellness. She is an avid cook and lover of wine. She lives with her husband, dogs, and cat on the water in beautiful League City, Texas, just outside of Houston in the United States.

Chapter 1
Introduction

> **Objectives**
> - Illustrate why this *Practical Guide* is different and unique from other resources available.
> - Describe the rationale and flow of the book.
> - Delineate how simple yet robust programs in occupational infection prevention can make a measurable difference in public health.

What's Different About This Book?

People working in healthcare settings sustain a higher incidence of occupational illness than any other industry sector (BLS 2017). This includes 20 million people (and rising yearly) that carry the risk of illnesses and infections that can affect all organs and organ systems, including the skin and respiratory systems, just by going to work. These occupational illnesses are most frequently caused by exposure to viruses, bacteria, and other microbiologic and physical irritants including influenza, multidrug-resistant organisms like MRSA, tuberculosis, respiratory viruses including coronaviruses like SARS-CoV-2, and physical splashes of blood and body fluids that can result in exposure to HIV and/or hepatitis C.

The winter of 2019/2020 will forever be known as the season that changed generations of people around the world. When SARS-CoV-2 emerged among patients with atypical pneumonia in China in December 2019, many public and occupational health practitioners became concerned. This will be discussed more in Chap. 11. The COVID-19 pandemic serves as an incredible illustration of the critical importance of careful attention on occupational infection prevention and its impact on global public health.

© Springer Nature Switzerland AG 2020

A. H. Mitchell, *Preventing Occupational Exposures to Infectious Disease in Health Care*, https://doi.org/10.1007/978-3-030-56039-3_1

In addition to biological hazards, occupational illness in health care like in other industries can also be caused by exposures to chemical and physical irritants like cleaners, detergents, disinfectants, sterilants, radiation, dusts, particulates and more; however exposures to infectious diseases tend to be the most serious and potentially devastating as a result of direct patient care.

With so much global focus on preventing similar types of exposures in patient populations and preventing healthcare-associated infections (HAIs), there is less focus on protecting those providing patient care from similarly devastating illnesses or infections.

This book serves as a practical guide for protecting workers from infectious disease. It serves as a reference for program design and implementation from an occupational infection prevention and control point of view. It serves as a roadmap, a recipe, or a blueprint – for building, maintaining, evaluating, and growing programs, policies, and campaigns designed to prevent occupational exposures to infectious disease in healthcare.

The guide is intended to be used by those with the greatest responsibility of all – protecting one of our most valuable assets, healthcare personnel. *Practical Guide* users may include professionals with job functions or tasks in occupational or employee health and safety, infection prevention and control, biological safety, infectious disease, risk management, and/or environmental health and safety in healthcare settings. The guide is meant to serve those with varying levels of experience in occupational health and/or occupational infection prevention. For those new to the role, background and fundamental information has been included to help you gain confidence as you ramp up in your role. For seasoned professionals, there are tools, resources, and ideas that are new and ready for you to roll out or pass along.

This book is not intended to sit dusty and sun bleached on a shelf, in a box, or to be used as a riser for a computer monitor. It is meant to be stained with coffee rings, its pages dog-eared with a book spine that opens and lays flat without even the slightest press. It is not only a "how to" but a when and where. And most importantly, it details the *why* and provides the real public health significance of building better, safer programs in health care that protect its workers from exposure to infectious and bloodborne disease that cause illness and infection and that have the potential to negatively impact patient and community care at a time when we need it most.

Ready-to-Use Information

Practical Guide readers will have ready-to-use information to either build a new occupational exposure prevention and control program or expand and revitalize an existing one. Not only is the reasoning behind building successful programs provided within these pages, but there are also sample programs, plans, campaigns or blitzes, and recordkeeping logs to use daily, weekly, monthly, or even as you update plans and policies annually.

The chapters that lay ahead are designed to serve as justification, form, function, and utility. They are laid out for quick reference, including information on what, when, how, and most importantly – why. The design and flow is built for success.

Chapters

- Public Health Significance
- Controlling and Preventing Occupational Illness and Infection
- Microbiology Basics
- Occupational Safety and Health Administration (OSHA) Regulatory Compliance
- Other Regulatory Requirements, National Standards, and Accreditation
- Performing a Hazard Assessment and Building an Exposure Control Plan
- Institutional and Administrative Controls
- Engineering Controls and Safer Medical Devices
- Personal Protective Equipment Placement and Use
- Facing a Modern Pandemic
- Making It All Work

Each chapter also provides practical information, education plans, and training materials, as well as implementation exercises and campaign tools.

Establishing Your Impact

Occupational infection prevention and control professionals are often called to task to defend or justify the reasons behind occupational health and safety and infection prevention and control programs. When resources are thin or a committee has been called to decide whether facility allocates funds to building a new diagnostics lab or add a much needed FTE in your department, you may find Chap. 2 Public Health Significance most useful to help you justify the need for ongoing support.

It doesn't help that programs of the past had the word "control" in the title: Infection "Control," Exposure "Control," and Damage "Control." There has been migration to substitute the term "control" for "prevention.": Infection "Prevention" and Exposure "Prevention" with damage control migrating to "Risk Management." A regular illustration to leadership to include what has been controlled, so that prevention can flourish. In other words, if we *control* a situation in the emergency department where personal protective equipment (PPE) is now immediately accessible to all personnel at every bedside, then we have averted (*prevented*) risk (a potential infectious outbreak).

This chapter includes the evidence base needed to not only defend a policy, program, action, or *control* to leadership, management, fellow colleagues, and staff but also to provide a solid grounding to establish why worker safety and health is critical to not only patient safety but to overarching facility safety, security, and even public health more broadly so that infectious crises and risk can be *prevented.*

While the information herein will be based on scientific rigor, evidence, and centuries of experience, peer-reviewed literature does not tell the whole story. Thanks to hundreds of years of dedication from the pioneers in worker safety and health – like Florence Nightingale, Alice Hamilton, Joseph Lister, even Benjamin Franklin, and so many others – and our governmental agencies like the National Institute for Occupational Safety and Health (NIOSH), the Occupational Safety and Health Administration (OSHA), the Environmental Protection Agency (EPA), and more, the scientific justification has been performed. Instituting the hierarchy of controls saves lives.

Decades of advancements in engineering controls like ventilation systems and high-efficiency particulate air (HEPA) filtration work to physically remove hazards from air. Barriers like personal protective equipment (PPE) when used properly halt microbes from moving from place to place and person to person. Annual employee training improves awareness and increases preventive skills. And who could be blinded to whether they are wearing a respirator or not? Or whether they are using a medical device with a safety mechanism or not? Or whether they've had a flu shot or not.

Providing Practical Information

The chapters ahead hold a host of practical information. They are proverbial recipes in a cookbook. Included are model plans, analyses, exposure incident logs, training elements, and more. Many elements can be copied and put in a three-ring binder or carried around in a hardy clipboard when doing rounds or going to committee meetings.

Model programs and plans:

- Exposure control plans
- Hazard control plans
- Job hazard analyses
- Sharps injury and blood/body fluid exposure logs
- Occupational infection prevention rounding checklist
- Cost-benefit modeling and more

These model programs and plans are drawn from key regulatory agencies like OSHA and EPA; credible research and clinical government centers like NIOSH and the CDC; national professional associations like the American Industrial Hygiene Association (AIHA), the American Society of Safety Engineers (ASSE), the Association for Professionals in Infection Control and Epidemiology (APIC), the Society for Healthcare Epidemiology of America (SHEA), the American Public Health Association (APHA), the Infectious Diseases Society of America (IDSA), the American Nurses' Association (ANA), the Association for Occupational Health

Professionals in Healthcare (AOHP), the Association for Biosafety and Biosecurity (ABSA), the National Fire Protection Agency (NFPA), and others; and organized labor and unions like the Service Employees International Union (SEIU), the American Federation of Governmental Employees (AFGE), the AFL-CIO, the American Federation of Teachers (AFT), and more.

Since there are more people from around the world accessing US healthcare organizations than ever before, increasing the potential for exposure to emerging and re-emerging infectious disease threats to healthcare workers, this guide will also provide sample programs and plans from global champion groups including the World Health Organization (WHO) and Médecins Sans Frontières (aka Doctors Without Borders).

It is important that once a plan is built and in action that it remains stoic and solid over time – it is the foundation on which all other safety programs are built. But in order to best suit the personnel and unique demands on your facility, it also needs to have the capability to flex and flow based on new standards, requirements, external threats, internal risks, or organizational changes. As such, these programs and plans are built with room to grow. In OSHA terms, they are "performance-based" plans and can be adjusted based on how well your organization is (or isn't) doing.

Utilizing Educational Plans and Training Modules

Not only do nearly all federal compliance standards require the development and execution of employee/staff education and training, but many also are offered to new employees at the time of hire (and transfer) and to all current employees at least annually. This is true not just for OSHA and EPA regulatory standards but also for Joint Commission and other accreditation and licensing organizations like state departments of health and public health.

If you are not a full-time educator or staff trainer, the development and rollout of these educational plans can be a daunting task. The educational resources in the guide will provide some educational plans and sample training modules for topic areas.

New Hire, Preplacement Training Let's say, for example, there is a new hire orientation training for professionals in the clinical diagnostics lab that will not be administering direct patient care. You know their background in microbiology is stronger than any other professional group entering the facility, so you can scale back on the plans and modules for that group and focus more on *Occupational Infectious Disease Risk*, *Regulatory Compliance*, and *PPE Placement and Use*. Then you can build implementation plans and evaluation tools around those units or maybe even have them help you build up the microbiology modules for others.

Seasonal or Ongoing Annual Training Or say you have a new group of medical residents arriving this summer and your facility just instituted several new safety-engineered devices and a revamped occupational infection prevention program, your orientation for them may include much more focus on Chaps. 9 and 10.

People learn differently. Some learn from seeing, some from hearing, some from reading, and some from doing. There are differences in how people learn from generation to generation, especially in workplaces like health care that may include employees from a span of three or four generations. Many like multimedia include paper, electronic, web-based, video, and classroom style approaches. PowerPoint lectures may leave your trainees with much to be desired and even more to learn once the session has concluded.

Trainees/staff need to provide not only you as a trainer with immediate feedback but also their peers, colleagues, and managers. They need to be able to express what works and what doesn't work. They need to learn in an environment that offers diversity, both of media and of peers, experiences, and backgrounds, to include mixed classes/courses/sessions where doctors, environmental services, and administrators learn altogether. You may yourself learn more by placing unlikely agents of change in one room.

What drives people to adapt safer practices, utilize controls, and improve compliance with PPE is unique to each individual. Your colleague's belief of risks to his or her own health is not the same as your beliefs about the risks to your health. Given all of the unique and independent drivers of human health, how you build educational and training modules with effective feedback loops will help to better develop, execute, and evaluate the programs in place to reduce even eliminate occupational exposures to infectious disease.

Implementing Exercises and Campaign Tools

Habits are not formed without practice, so there are "R2P" (research to practice) and "P2P" (policy to practice) exercises included to incorporate with staff and leadership during blitzes, campaigns, committee meetings, new hire orientation, annual training, or during those important XYZ days or weeks of the year, like Infection Prevention Week, Occupational Safety and Health Week, World MRSA Day, World TB Day, or Infectious Disease Week.

In this guide, content can be pulled to include in educational elements and provision of tools and resources can be used to turn those into immediate action.

Oftentimes, the key to building a culture of safety that results in an everyday, ongoing climate of safety is the need for "management buy-in" in order to build and sustain programs of importance that become part of the organization's personality, essential to its infrastructure. Sometimes this results in a chicken and egg cyclical logic – what comes first: management buy-in to build safer occupational programs or successes from safer occupational programs that results in management buy-in? This is covered in great detail in Chap. 8, Institutional Controls.

Implementation exercises are tools to use so that practice makes perfect. Doing something the right way over and over again results in a good habit. A habit that results in an avoided risk and in the case of this *Practical Guide*, a non-transmission, a nonevent of an infectious disease or pathogenic organism of HIV or hepatitis C or influenza to your cherished staff, colleagues, and friends. There is so much focus on patient safety in healthcare and rightly so. These exercises are intended to remind institutions that preventing transmission from patient to worker also works to prevent transmission from worker back to patient.

Break the Cycle of One, Break the Cycle of All!

Contaminated hands of healthcare personnel are most frequently cited as the vector of transmission of microorganisms that cause HAIs in hospital patient and long-term care resident populations. In 2020, the world also learned about how viable pathogens like SARS-CoV-2 can be in the environment and how important constant attention to handwashing is. It has been a frequently identified critical step in patient safety, but what was less frequently identified however is how contaminated hands of healthcare personnel can result in their own exposure.

This may be because workers are essentially healthier than the patients they care for. There is something that exists in occupational health called the "healthy worker effect" (Last 1995).

> Healthy Worker Effect (HWE) is a phenomenon initially observed in studies of occupational diseases: Workers usually exhibit lower overall death rates than the general population because the severely ill and chronically disabled are ordinarily excluded from employment

With the average age of nurses edging toward the mid-50s and health, even in working populations, becoming more and more compromised from obesity, diabetes, chronic stress and inflammation, joint ailments, and more, the healthy worker effect may hold less of a protective factor than in the decades to come.

Imagining the Transfer of Microbes

Imagine if you would that a microbe is visible to the naked eye. Pretend it is illuminated, and it is sitting on Mr. Jones' skin, right near a peripheral IV inserted in his forearm.

A nurse goes in to attend to Mr. Jones, and she touches his skin (not even doing anything clinical, just to say hi and ask how he is doing). She thinks nothing of it simply because she isn't doing a clinical procedure like changing a dressing or administering IV medications. She then has a tickle and a twitch and rubs her nose as she exits the room and heads over to the nurses' station. Now that illuminated little pathogen is potentially in her nasal (mucous) membrane. If she is healthy, not a big deal; maybe she becomes colonized without any symptoms or illness, maybe not. Now that nurse moves to her next patient or Mr. Jones' wife or his/her newborn

Fig. 1.1 Potential contamination
and transmission cycle

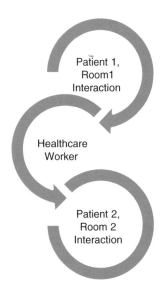

baby at home and does the same slight, gentle touch, the microbe then potentially moves to her or him or them. You get the point.

You don't know how far that hitchhiker or its colony are going to travel. You also don't know the relative sickness or wellness of whomever it is upon which it will land. It is how outbreaks occur in single departments/units/wards. It doesn't make the healthy people sick, but it sure does make the unhealthy people sick or sicker, ill or more ill, or colonized to infected status.

That's why preventing the *first* exposure from the patient to the worker can prevent *all* downstream exposures (Fig. 1.1). If the focus is there first, there is not much else to do to break that chain, and efforts can be asserted to other critically important tasks. It is at this point in time when appropriate glove use, don- and doffing time and process, and adequate handwashing or hand hygiene need to happen. It is most critical at ground zero. This is the foundation of standard precautions and subsequently the foundation of occupational health and safety as it relates to exposure or infection prevention.

Tools and Resources

Finally, in the box of tools in the coming chapters, there are comprehensive lists of online/web-based resources, documents, guidelines, standards, regulations, and outreach materials from professional societies, trade organizations, unions, regulatory agencies, research firms, advocacy sites, networking email listservs, and surveillance systems to name a few.

Gain access to these if more background or information is needed about research methods, scientific rigor, population-based statistics, and in-depth microbiology or simply if you want to expand your own knowledge and keep abreast of more current information as it is released. Use the tools supplied in the Appendices to dive deep if you need to, especially for plan building and hazard control. This *Practical Guide*, while providing a great deal of depth, is only the tip of the iceberg. The tip of the iceberg provides the greatest gems, think diamond tip, but you will frequently need more.

This *Practical Guide* is designed to be a personal assistant, to serve as a faithful companion on your journey leading your institution toward the elimination of occupational exposure to infectious and bloodborne disease. It will help you to weave the yarn of occupational health and safety and infection prevention into the loom of healthcare practice with all personnel, every process, every procedure, every patient, every time, every day.

This guide has been crafted with careful thought and cherished guidance and is fueled by passion for those who protect people while they care for others.

After all, there is no health care without healthcare workers.

References

Bureau of Labor Statistics, SNR07. Illness cases by category of illness - rates, counts, and percent - industry division – 2017

Last, J. (1995). *A dictionary of epidemiology* (3rd ed.). Oxford, UK: Oxford University Press.

Chapter 2
Public Health Significance

Objectives
- Discuss why occupational exposure to infectious diseases in health care is an important public health issue.
- List and discuss microorganisms most likely to cause occupational illness or infection.
- Describe why preventing occupational illness and infection is critical to improving healthcare quality.

Occupational Exposure Today

Occupational exposure to infectious disease is as relevant today as ever it has been. The 1980s brought the fear of acquired immunodeficiency syndrome (AIDS) as well as an increased incidence of hepatitis B and C infection which resulted in the development of universal and then standard precautions which dictate that healthcare personnel assume all blood and body fluids have the potential to carry bloodborne diseases. This practice simplified protective factors because no matter the patient and no matter their state of infectivity, they were treated the same.

Today, there are almost 20 million Americans employed by the US healthcare sector and employment growth in this field far surpasses all other economic sectors, with projections for growth approximately 20% from 2014 and 2024 (BLS 2018, BLS 2019). With more people employed in health care than in decades past and an unbearably high prevalence of current and emerging infectious and bloodborne disease, taking steps to prevent occupational transmission is critical to overall public health. In 2020, the world began to experience the devastating impact a pandemic like SARS-CoV-2 can have on whole populations of people. For the first time in a long time, our focus on the importance of protecting healthcare workers and other

© Springer Nature Switzerland AG 2020
A. H. Mitchell, *Preventing Occupational Exposures to Infectious Disease in Health Care*, https://doi.org/10.1007/978-3-030-56039-3_2

essential personnel came into view. Highlighting deficiencies in healthcare systems' abilities to protect their workforce at a level necessary became a highly publicized political and public health blame game. Ultimately, it unveiled a global public health problem, which is the under-resourcing and under-valuing of occupational health preparedness.

In its 2015 Policy Statement "Preventing Occupational Transmission of Globally Emerging Infectious Disease Threats," APHA Occupational Health and Safety section authors state that "(h)ospital and public health preparedness for globally emerging infectious disease is an ongoing public health priority. Protecting U.S. healthcare workers and other workers who must respond to infectious disease outbreaks that arise from transmission in their communities is a pivotal link in creating an effective public health preparedness program" (APHA 2015).

Since there are hundreds of microorganisms that can cause illness or infection in humans (pathogenic organisms), this guide will cover the highest prevalence organisms that affect healthcare workers. Depending on where you live and work in the world, these may be different for you and the employees in your healthcare setting. The World Health Organization (WHO) has useful online resources on infectious disease available on their "Infectious Disease" topics page of their website at www.who.int.

Essentially microorganisms that can cause illness or infection – pathogens – are transmitted by "vectors." Many people consider vectors small organisms like flies, mosquitoes, and ticks that can carry disease like Zika or Lyme disease, and when they bite a person, the disease can be transmitted. As it relates to the healthcare environment, vectors also include contaminated hands, patient care items (e.g., blood pressure cuffs, stethoscopes), medical devices (e.g., IV infusion connectors, endoscopes, surgical instruments), and contaminated surfaces or textiles (e.g., uniforms, lab coats, sinks, toilets, bedrails, etc.).

The degree of contamination and the length of viability (organism or part of organism is living or able to infect) varies greatly based on the circumstance, type of microorganism and type of surface, humidity, air flow, and how frequently it is touched and/or moved from place to place. A chart like this may be a useful tool for identifying what surfaces in a facility need to be considered as potential sources (risks) of cross-transmission and subsequently addressed by clinical and environmental services personnel for cleaning and disinfection protocols (Table 2.1).

A few viruses may dissipate and die in the air where several milliliters of sputum with hearty bacteria may live for hours or days. For example, there is a big

Table 2.1 Examples of healthcare surface types and the potential for cross-contamination based on portability

	Non-porous hard surfaces	Porous soft surfaces
Fixed	I. Typical high touch: sinks, counters, lightswitches, floors	IV. Floor and wall covering upholstery, couches
Portable	II. Tables, charts, carts, hard chairs/ furniture	V. Upholstery, chairs, curtains, linen
Mobile	III. Stethoscope, diagnostic testing supplies, respiratory equipment	VI. Blood pressure cuff, patient gowns, apparel, scrubs, lab coats

difference in the viability of a virus when someone who is sick sneezes in the hallway of an emergency department compared to the bacterial load and potential for transmission for contamination on soft surfaces like upholstered chair arms in an emergency department waiting room. The viral load from the person that sneezes in the air can dissipate and die quickly if it never reaches a surface and/or heavy sputum falls to the floor, but the upholstered chair serves as a comfortable media for bacteria to live, even thrive, until the next person who sits in the chair comes into contact with it.

We did learn more about the viability of viruses in the air during the COVID-19 pandemic. It seems the original "6-foot" physical distancing rule came from a paper published in 1934 (Wells 1934). It astutely illustrated how larger droplets drop to the ground/floor, but smaller ones can circulate in the air within an approximate 6-foot radius. This was a scientific certainty nearly 90 years ago. In addition, during the 1918 Spanish flu, public health authorities recommended physical distancing and increased air flow which among other similar actions to COVID-19 today influenced the "flattening of the curve" until it ended within 2 years.

Bloodborne Pathogens

Human Immunodeficiency Virus (HIV)

According to the CDC, approximately 1.2 million persons aged 13 and older living in the United States were living with HIV infection, and 1 in 7 are unaware of their diagnosis (CDC 2016a). While the diagnosis of new infections has declined since 2012, patients with unidentified HIV still represent a substantial risk to healthcare personnel who sustain a contaminated needlestick or splash or splatter of blood or blood-contaminated body fluids to mucus membranes or non-intact or abraded skin.

Acquired Immunodeficiency Syndrome (AIDS)

AIDS is the most advanced stage of HIV. Many times, the terms HIV and AIDS are comingled. However, most people that have HIV do not have or will likely never develop AIDS if they seek treatment soon after becoming diagnosed. AIDS is signified by an immune system that is so weakened that it does not have the ability to fight off certain kinds of infections and cancers, such as "PCP (a type of pneumonia) or KS (Kaposi sarcoma, a type of cancer that affects the skin and internal organs), wasting syndrome (involuntary weight loss), memory impairment, or tuberculosis." (VA 2018)

As it relates to occupational exposure from a patient or source blood from a person with AIDS, risk may be higher than from someone with HIV because the viral load (particles per mL of blood) of virus is higher. This can result in a greater

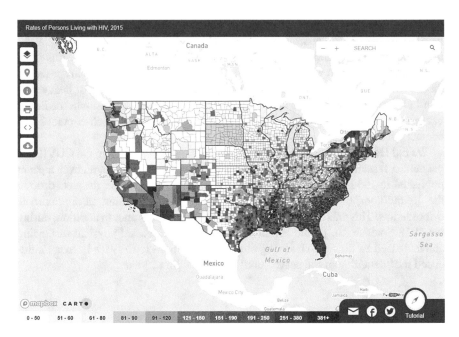

Fig. 2.1 Rates of persons living with HIV (AIDSVu 2016). (Reprinted with permission)

likelihood of transmission if there is a needlestick, contaminated sharp injury, or blood exposure to mucus membranes or non-intact skin.

In order to determine what prevalence rates are in specific regions of the United States, AIDSVu provides information based on data reported through the states to the Centers for Disease Prevention and Control (CDC) (Fig. 2.1).

Hepatitis B Virus (HBV)

It is estimated that in the United States alone, more than 2.2 million people are suffering with chronic HBV infection (CDC 2014). Globally, HBV is endemic with up to 18% of many countries' citizens living with the disease (CDC 2016b). Due to the globalization of travel and increasing access of unvaccinated foreign nationals seeking US health care, the risk of hepatitis B virus (HBV) is also on the rise. While today, children are required to be vaccinated for HBV prior to entering school, it is unknown how long immunity lasts into adulthood, and with recent anti-vaccine campaigns, immunity to HBV is waning.

Chronic HBV is an underlying cause of liver cancer with the HBV vaccine once touted as the first "cancer vaccine." The vaccine by nature of its effectiveness could prevent the onset of HBV given an exposure, thus preventing seroconversion to hepatitis infection and subsequent onset of liver cancer.

Hepatitis C Virus (HCV)

The prevalence of bloodborne infection, illness, and disease is unacceptably high both in the United States and around the world. Hepatitis C virus (HCV) prevalence has actually increased dramatically. This bloodborne pathogen disease increased more than 150% between 2010 and 2013 (Dan 2016)! Approximately three million Americans are infected with HCV (CDC 2017).

In fact, the CDC report that more baby boomers (those born between 1946 and 1964) die from hepatitis C than from 60 other infectious diseases combined (CDC 2013)! Baby boomers (1945–1965) are five times more likely to have a HCV infection than any other age group most likely because there was a lack of awareness of the importance of universal precautions in the time period between the 1960s through the 1980s. This poses an increasing risk to healthcare personnel than in previous years because this age group is entering the healthcare system more frequently.

Overall, three in four people do not know they are infected with HCV and therefore do not get the medical care they need. This also means that since they do not know they are infected, they can be a potential source of occupational risk to those who may come into contact with their blood or body fluids during regular doctor or dentist office visits.

The CDC provides national maps that indicate the estimated number of people living with hepatitis C virus each year (Fig. 2.2).

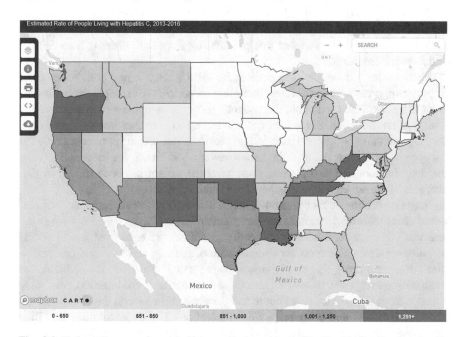

Fig. 2.2 Estimated rates of people living with hepatitis C (HepVu 2016). (Reprinted with permission)

There are many useful videos and factsheets for bloodborne disease including:

- 5 Things to Know about TB Video (CDC) https://www.youtube.com/watch?v=wA_fObLY6GE
- Hepatitis C Fact Sheet (CDC) https://www.cdc.gov/knowmorehepatitis/media/PDFs/FactSheet-boomers.pdf
- HIV and Viral Hepatitis (CDC) https://www.cdc.gov/hiv/pdf/library/factsheets/hiv-viral-hepatitis.pdf
- Occupational HIV Transmission and Prevention among Health Care Workers (CDC) https://www.cdc.gov/hiv/pdf/workplace/cdc-hiv-healthcareworkers.pdf

Co-infection and Multidrug-Resistant Pathogens

One occupational exposure can result in potential transmission of multiple pathogens.

If bloodborne diseases like HIV and HCV are identified and treated, they are considered more chronic diseases now; meaning that people who are diagnosed or live with the diseases can live a long and health life and do not necessarily die from them. This poses interesting and unique situations, where they enter healthcare facilities frequently as patients (in- or out-patient or in doctors' offices or clinics) and as such are at increased likelihood of acquiring a secondary pathogen that can lead to infection including methicillin-resistant *Staphylococcus aureus* (MRSA). Additionally, approximately 25% of those infected with HIV are also co-infected with HCV and 10% are also co-infected with HBV (CDC 2016). People living with multiple infections are at tripled risk of suffering from liver disease, liver failure, and liver-related death.

Many healthcare facilities test patients for MRSA colonization or infection prior to performing medical procedures, including surgeries, for example, because they want to be well informed about the patient's risk of developing a complication like a surgical site infection. Some facilities will test all patients that are admitted so that they can put those patients on isolation precautions. Precautions protect not only the patient him or herself but also the healthcare workers caring for them and anyone that may be admitted to that same room after the patient has been moved or discharged. There are champions and critics to both approaches.

Very few healthcare facilities however do active surveillance testing for occupational cases of MRSA colonization or infection in healthcare personnel for many reasons. The most common is that identifying MRSA presence may result in complications with requirements for decolonization, staffing, and workers' compensation. For example, if a physician was tested positive for MRSA or methicillin-susceptible *Staphylococcus aureus* (MSSA) colonization, are they excused from their duties to go home and decolonize for several days? Do they go about their duties and wear respiratory protection? If they decolonize and then recolonize, do they have to go about it all over again? Does the healthcare facility pay for this? Workers' compensation?

Due to many of these factors, multidrug-resistant organisms' (MDROs) prevalence among personnel is relatively unknown even though carriage is strongly associated with subsequent infection and illness. However, a few studies have been performed identifying MRSA among professions such as emergency services, nurses, and surgeons. Colonization rates range from 4.6% to 22.5% for emergency and first responders and 3.4–4.6% for health workers (Albrich and Harbarth 2008; Stevenson 2012; Orellana et al. 2016). As nearly no healthcare facility tests its personnel for colonization or infection with a multidrug-resistant organism, our ability to accurately estimate the burden and impact on workers is extremely limited. We know much more about the prevalence of these organisms in patient populations, and even then – due to extreme differences in testing practices from facility to facility – we know less than we should about risk.

Colonization rates can differ based on a healthcare practitioners' level of experience and expertise. In a study comparing patients to surgeons (residents and attending) in orthopedic settings, patients had lower rates of both MRSA and MSSA compared to surgeons, and residents had higher prevalence of MSSA than their attending surgical counterparts (Schwartzkopf et al. 2010). Patients had 18% colonization with MSSA compared to 35.7% of surgeons (59% of which were residents). For MRSA, 2.17% patients were colonized compared to 1.5% of surgeons (0% residents, 2.7% attendings).

Vaccine-Preventable Diseases

Measles

In the last several years, there has been a potentially destructive trend of parents not vaccinating their children from infectious diseases that have been vaccine-preventable for decades. Some of these decisions are based on religion or country of origin, some on preference, but many based on high media visibility, discredited research that there is a link between vaccines and autism in children. Whatever the case, it is having a negative impact on public health overall, as well as occupational health in health care.

States in the Pacific Northwest and Midwest like Washington, Oregon, and Wisconsin have seen the outbreaks of diseases like measles, rates that exceed those from more than 30 years. Transmission and infection are higher than in decades past due to the domestic "anti-vax" movement, which is amplified by unvaccinated travelers that enter the United States. Since measles has been reintroduced as an occupational pathogen of importance and frequently healthcare workers are the first in line to receive patients with known or suspected measles, it is important to have documentation of vaccination (two doses) and/or immunity.

The CDC attributed more than 30 cases of measles to exposure to two patients in Colorado who traveled to countries with endemic measles transmission (CDC 2018). The cases were transmitted and acquired during normal life activities like grocery shopping, schooling, and dining and in the patients' residences. The agency estimated that these cases cost almost $70,000 in disease investigation alone. Even single episodes of measles require a full-fledged public health response and can cost between $5000 to more than $180,000. There have been many measles outbreaks similar to this in dozens of states, including one recently of 134 cases in CA resulting from a visit to Disneyland (Miller 2015).

New York City experienced its largest measles outbreak in 30 years in 2018. This included 654 people who were infected with 52 hospitalized. Nearly 75% of those individuals were unvaccinated (CDC 2019a, b). Amazingly, of all measles cases in 2019, 75% were in New York.

Measles can be devastating to immunocompromised people resulting in pneumonia and/or encephalitis. Since it mimics the common cold or even COVID-19 (runny nose, cough, fever), someone infected with measles may not know they have it unless they have been tested for it specifically. Since measles can cause rash and conjunctivitis, it may only be when these symptoms are present that a person would seek out medical treatment and be tested.

Mumps

There have also been spikes of mumps in the United States over the last 10 years. Mumps is easily spread in close environments like schools, sports teams, dorms, and residential care facilities. Mumps is viral, so it can be transmitted from one person to the next via contact or air with saliva and/or mucus from an infected person. Since the mumps vaccine is frequently paired with measles and rubella, the increased incidence is not surprising given increased migration of foreign nationals to the United States and dipping immunization rates.

If diseases like measles, mumps, or rubella progress in a person and effect organ systems like the lungs, they can cause fever, conjunctivitis (pink eye), and other symptoms that can result in hospitalization and subsequently potentially affect other patients or healthcare personnel. If patients are not put on contact or isolation precautions while awaiting confirmatory diagnostics, they can serve as a vector for transmission. Vaccines work to prevent the spread of these preventable diseases so that they do not continue to become menaces to public health and the prosperity of our national economy.

Influenza

Many healthcare facilities of all types and sizes require employees to get the influenza vaccine every year. This is especially important for employees and healthcare personnel in acute and long-term care facilities because immunocompromised people including those that are very young, very old, or very sick are considered "high-risk" and are especially susceptible to acquiring and dying from the flu.

It is estimated that each year approximately 80–90% of flu related deaths occur in those 65 years or older. Personnel that work in long-term or post-acute care facilities like nursing homes and rehabilitation facilities need to be diligent about getting vaccinated so that they themselves do not become a potential vector to their patients, residents, or clients. While the flu vaccine's effectiveness does vary from year to year depending on the types and numbers of strains that are included in the vaccine itself, preventing the spread of even one or two strains is better than none at all. Nearly all healthcare facilities require that employees receive a flu vaccine every year. Each workplace has different protocols to address employees that refuse vaccine from a requirement of employment (termination) to wearing a surgical face mask or appropriate face covering during their work shift. We have learned much more about this during the COVID-19 pandemic and will continue to learn more when vaccines are available for emerging and emerged diseases. It is crucial to know the immunization laws in your state.

Tuberculosis (TB)

The World Health Organization estimates that TB is one of the top ten leading causes of death in the world (WHO 2017). It affects mostly adults in their productive and working years. It is the leading killer of people with HIV. Multidrug-resistant TB (MDRTB) is at public health crisis levels because of poor adherence to antimicrobial stewardship programs, delays in diagnosis and treatment, and poor management of drugs and supply of medications around the world (WHO 2017; CDC 2016). It is also exacerbated in crowded living or working conditions. TB can unduly affect warm climate countries with a large population like India, the Philippines, and Nigeria, but CDC estimates that one-third of the world's population is infected with TB (WHO 2017; CDC 2016).

In the United States as with other countries around the world, there is an influx of patients that either travel to high prevalence TB countries or people that emigrate or are refugees accessing care in countries other than their own. This makes TB a high likelihood bacterial pathogen of risk for those working in health care.

Available guidance from CDC recommends TB screening for healthcare personnel if there is occupational risk or ongoing exposure (CDC 2019a, b). Treatment is encouraged for all healthcare personnel with latent TB infection and ongoing annual education about TB risk factors.

Ultimately, there are a dozen of more vaccine-preventable diseases that can impact healthcare workers and should be a necessary part of any occupational infection prevention program. Just a few are listed here, but others include pertussis, varicella, meningococcal, and more. CDC and the Advisory Committee on Immunization Practices (ACIP) provide recommendations for all of them (CDC 2017).

At the writing of this book, a SARS-CoV-2 vaccine is in development. Once it is effective and available, what might a global uptake look like? Will it become mandatory for working populations? Will OSHA require it as they do the HBV vaccine? Will it become mandatory for immunocompromised people who want to venture out in public spaces? Will it become mandatory for all residents in nursing homes? Will it be required when someone is diagnosed with type 2 diabetes or heart disease? Will anti-vaxxers refuse to get it, and will a pandemic forever become endemic? This is an interesting period in global public health, one that will be telling for the safest future possible for those with underlying chronic disease at risk for secondary infections and illnesses, especially.

Emerging (and Emerged) Infectious Diseases

Recent global outbreaks and epidemics of emerging infectious diseases, including recent outbreaks of Ebola and Zika viruses, reinforce the need for preventing blood exposures to the healthcare workforce, patients, and communities. The cases of transmission of Ebola in the Dallas, Texas, region in 2014 reminded healthcare institutions that not only it is important to wear PPE as a means of protection, but it is also crucial to know how to remove contaminated PPE safely and in correct order so as not to cross-contaminate oneself upon removal or doffing.

Lessons learned from and preparations for these pathogens pale in comparison to what we have experienced and are continuing to experience from the SARS-CoV-2 pandemic and associated COVID-19 disease crisis. Never before in five generations have we experienced an infectious disease as life-changing as pandemic influenza of 1918 Spanish flu. The 1918 Spanish flu infected about 500 million people – about one-third of the world's population at the time with approximately 50 million deaths worldwide and 675,000 in the United States (CDC The Deadly Virus). (Note: For the purposes of this *Practical Guide*, with numbers of cases and deaths so fluid, providing a number would not be useful.)

COVID-19 has emerged, and because it is a novel virus that the human body does not have the capacity to fight off effectively, it is fierce. For those with critical symptoms, requiring hospitalization and mechanical ventilation, it is proving to be the most prevalent cause of death in the United States. The disease is exacerbated by underlying health conditions also prevalent among Americans including heart disease, high blood pressure, diabetes, chronic inflammation, autoimmune disorders, cancer, and other comorbidities.

Despite preparedness and stockpiling of PPE in US healthcare organizations during the H1N1 swine flu epidemic in 2009 and Ebola in 2013, we find desperately low to no availability of appropriate respiratory protection (filtering facepiece respirators like disposable N95s or reusable elastomerics) in many US cities like New York City and New Orleans. In addition to lack of availability of PPE, there is also lack of robust training for putting on (donning) and taking off (doffing) equipment that can result in undue risk. More about the current COVID-19 pandemic can be found in Chap. 11.

Several studies have been published in the peer-reviewed literature quantifying the risk of cross-/self-contamination during doffing PPE (especially gloves and gowns) and estimate that sometimes self-transmission can occur as more than 50% of the time (Pyrek 2018; Suen et al. 2018; Tomas et al. 2015).

Understanding the risks associated with occupational exposures to infectious disease and importance of putting proper controls in place is why this book is being written. Zika has already been documented and transmitted via needlestick in a clinical laboratory setting. The resurgence of vaccine-preventable diseases, like measles and HBV as mentioned, means that risks are not only uncertain but also potentially increasing today compared to the 1980s.

Patients with known or unknown bloodborne disease accessing any type of healthcare facility, especially non-acute care locations like specialty offices and clinics, present a grave risk to healthcare personnel if appropriate controls are not in place to prevent occupational exposure to blood and body fluids.

Disaster-Related Illnesses

Whether you are a believer in climate change or not, Mother Nature can be cruel, and she is seeming to be more frequently cruel now more than ever. Hurricanes, floods, fires, earthquakes, tsunamis, monsoons, and blizzards bring with them sometimes unexpected risks – one that we may not be prepared for but must consider. As it relates to infectious disease, depending where you are in the world, that could mean exposure to cholera, West Nile virus, dengue fever, hepatitis, and rabies to name a

---

Box 2.1 Disaster-Related Risks

Disasters that bring about increased risk to infectious agents can result in a few different scenarios involving risk:

- Workers become exposed in their communities and potentially pose a transmissible risk to co-workers and/or patients.
- Patients are exposed during or after the event in their communities and can transmit pathogens when they access healthcare systems.
- Members of the community can become contaminated or infected during cleanup activities.
- The healthcare environment and/or grounds themselves can become contaminated with pathogenic organisms.

Box 2.2 Natural Disaster Preparedness and Response Resources
- OSHA Emergency Preparedness and Response https://www.osha.gov/SLTC/emergencypreparedness/
- NIEHS Emergency Response https://www.niehs.nih.gov/health/topics/population/response/index.cfm
- NIOSH Emergency Response Resources https://www.cdc.gov/niosh/topics/emres/natural.html
- WHO Flooding and Communicable Diseases Fact Sheet http://www.who.int/hac/techguidance/ems/flood_cds/en/   World   Health   Organization (WHO). (n.d.).

few. Rising waters, fires, and displaced earth force animals out of their habitats, create disastrous sewage spills, and create situations where your working population may have exposures to any number of bloodborne, vector-borne, or infectious diseases. Box 2.1 provides unique challenges about increased occupational risk to be considered during disasters, and Box 2.2 provides useful resources for risk mitigation.

University of Texas identifies in its *Nine Habits for a Highly Effective Disaster Recovery* that healthcare organizations must "champion excellent medical care for all" (University of Texas at Austin 2017). Everyone is suffering during a time like this, and excellent care can include not just medical care for patients but potentially medical care for your employees if they become ill or infected during or after a natural disaster.

Whatever the case and whomever the "patient," it is important to be prepared. OSHA, NIOSH, NIEHS (National Institute of Environmental Health Sciences), Centers for Disease Control and Prevention (CDC), and World Health Organization (WHO) offer great resources to help you and your teams build systems and procedures for safer working environments during and after natural disasters that may impact a higher likelihood that workers are exposed to infectious disease.

While these resources are built for all safety precautions during emergencies and disaster cleanup and remediation including physical and health hazards, each of them has pearls of wisdom specific to preventing occupational exposure to infectious disease. You may want to share these with your colleagues in risk management and environmental health and safety if they do not already have them.

References

AIDSVu. (2016). *Rates of people living with HIV, 2016*. https://map.aidsvu.org/map

Albrich, W. C., & Harbarth, S. (2008). Health-care workers: Source, vector, or victim of MRSA? *The Lancet Infectious Diseases., 8*(5), 289–301.

American Public Health Association (APHA). (2015, November). *Preventing occupational transmission of globally emerging infectious disease threats*. Policy Statement.

Bureau of Labor Statistics. (2018). *Employment by major industry sector, 2018.* https://www.bls.gov/emp/tables/employment-by-major-industry-sector.htm

Bureau of Labor Statistics. (2019). *Healthcare occupations, 2019.* https://www.bls.gov/ooh/healthcare/home.htm

CDC. (2013). *Hepatitis C. Testing Baby Boomers Saves Lives.*

CDC. (2014). *Surveillance for Viral Hepatitis – United States, 2014.* https://www.cdc.gov/hepatitis/statistics/2014surveillance/commentary.htm

CDC. (2016, May). *Recommended vaccines for healthcare workers.* https://www.cdc.gov/vaccines/adults/rec-vac/hcw.html

CDC. (2016a). *HIV Surveillance Report.*

CDC. (2017). *ACIP Vaccine Recommendations and Guidelines.*

CDC. (2018). *Measles cases and outbreaks.* https://www.cdc.gov/measles/cases-outbreaks.html

CDC. (2019a, May). *Tuberculosis infection control in health care settings.* https://www.cdc.gov/tb/topic/infectioncontrol/default.htm

CDC. (2019b). *Tuberculosis testing and treatment of US health care personnel.* https://www.cdc.gov/nchhstp/newsroom/images/multimedia/tb/HCP-TB-recommendations-highres.jpg

CDC. *Public health economic burden associated with two single measles case investigations — Colorado, 2016–2017.* https://www.cdc.gov/mmwr/volumes/66/wr/mm6646a3.htm?s_cid=mm6646a3_e

Dan, E. (2016). Institute of Medicine expert committee assessing feasibility of viral hepatitis elimination targets in the U.S. HCV Advocate. http://hepatitisc.hcvadvocate.org/tag/cdc

Department of Veterans Affairs. (2018). What is AIDS?

HepVu. (2016). *Rates of people living with hepatitis C, 2016.* https://hepvu.org/map/

Miller, L. (2015). Colorado department of public health and environment. *Measles Update.* https://www.childrensimmunization.org/uploads/Measles-Miller-Trefren-Provider-Ed-April-2015.pdf

Orellana, R., et al. (2016). Methicillin-resistant *Staphylococcus aureus* in Ohio EMS providers: A statewide cross-sectional study. *Prehospital Emergency Care, 20*(2), 184.

Pyrek, K. (2018, July). PPE donning and doffing reveals gaps in knowledge and practice. *Infection Control Today.*

Schwartzkopf, R., et al. (2010). Prevalence of Staphylococcus aureus colonization in orthopaedic surgeons and their patients a prospective cohort controlled study. *The Journal of Bone and Joint Surgery, 92*(9), 1815–1819.

Stevenson, K., et al. (2012, October). Reduction of MRSA colonization in EMS personnel and equipment to prevent secondary injury in Ohio trauma patients. Ohio Division of EMS Injury Prevention Research Grant.

Suen, L. K. P., et al. (2018). Self-contamination during doffing of personal protective equipment by healthcare workers to prevent Ebola transmission. *Antimicrobial Resistance & Infection Control, 7,* 157.

Tomas, M., et al. (2015). Contamination of health care personnel during removal of personal protective equipment. *JAMA Internal Medicine, 175*(12), 1904–1910.

University of Texas at Austin. (2017). *Nine habits for a highly effective disaster recovery.* https://news.utexas.edu/2017/11/03/nine-habits-for-a-highly-effective-disaster-recovery

Wells, W. F. (1934). On Air-borne infection. Study II. Droplets and droplet nuclei. *Stokes' Mathematical and Physical Papers, 1^01, 3,* 60.

WHO. (2017). *Tuberculosis.* http://www.who.int/mediacentre/factsheets/fs104/en/

World Health Organization (WHO). (n.d.). *Flooding and communicable diseases fact sheet.* http://www.who.int/hac/techguidance/ems/flood_cds/en/

Chapter 3
Controlling and Preventing Occupational Illness and Infection

Objectives
- Identify critical elements in an occupational infection prevention and control plan.
- Describe important employee vaccination and immunization plans.
- Outline the concept of the industrial hygiene hierarchy of controls.
- Provide information on workers' rights.

Introduction

Infectious disease outbreak, epidemic, and pandemic events occur in waves that remind health systems in nations around the world that maintaining high levels of preparedness for unexpected biological events and global health security is important. From the uncertainties of the early AIDS epidemics in San Francisco and New York in the 1980s in the U.S. to scares of bioterrorism in a post-9/11 America, to avian influenza in the 2000s; to actual occupational transmission of Ebola in Dallas, Texas, in 2014; and to the 2020 pandemic of COVID-19, it is too risky to let our guard down. Considering and preparing for what potential exposures that result in unforeseen impacts is a critical element of public health.

Every time there is an outbreak or scare of an outbreak, there are federal and state monies available for "ramping up" stockpiles of personal protective equipment (PPE), vaccines, and other supplies necessary to mitigate the infectious agent of interest. Experience has taught us, especially during the Ebola and COVID-19 crises, that remaining in a constant state of preparedness is important for every patient, every procedure, every time.

If a person feels unwell and does not trust in their ability to drive or is simply so unwell that they cannot drive, they call 911. An ambulance is dispatched to their location to transport them to the nearest hospital. During the journey, there are many

© Springer Nature Switzerland AG 2020
A. H. Mitchell, *Preventing Occupational Exposures to Infectious Disease in Health Care*, https://doi.org/10.1007/978-3-030-56039-3_3

healthcare personnel along the way that can be exposed to whatever pathogen is ailing that person (now a patient).

Risk is open to first responders, paramedics, emergency medical services personnel, triage personnel, emergency department personnel, patients and families in the waiting room, and more. While the patient and their providers await confirmatory diagnostic test results, they may not be afforded the correct type of contact or isolation precautions. This provides an enormous window for the likelihood of transmitting the microbe or microbes causing the patient to be unwell. These windows are where protective screens are needed and are why standard precautions are in place. Unfortunately, according to occupational incident surveillance, they are not being used as frequently as necessary. The International Safety Center's Exposure Prevention Information Network (EPINet®) has been tracking occupational exposures to blood and body fluids since the early 1990s. According to 2019 data, nearly 60% of splashes or splatters of blood and body fluids were to a healthcare personnel's eyes, nose, or mouth (mucous membranes), and of those less than 7% were wearing eye protection, a mask or respirator, faceshield, or another face-appropriate PPE (EPINet 2019).

Mucous membrane exposures are considered extremely high risk. A single incident can result in exposure to multiple pathogens because of the increased prevalence of co-infection among many patients (people infected with more than one infectious disease). The conjunctiva of the eye is extremely vessel rich and the protective layering of the eye can easily be compromised from allergy, contacts, makeup, infection, or other conditions resulting in a higher likelihood of disease transmission (Fig. 3.1).

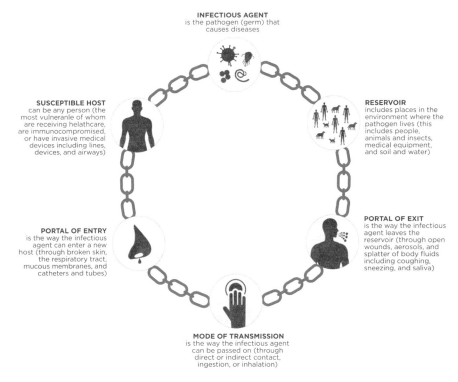

INFECTIOUS AGENT
is the pathogen (germ) that causes diseases

SUSCEPTIBLE HOST
can be any person (the most vulneranle of whom are receiving helathcare, are immunocompromised, or have invasive medical devices including lines, devices, and airways)

RESERVOIR
includes places in the environment where the pathogen lives (this includes people, animals and insects, medical equipment, and soil and water)

PORTAL OF ENTRY
is the way the infectious agent can enter a new host (through broken skin, the respiratory tract, mucous membranes, and catheters and tubes)

PORTAL OF EXIT
is the way the infectious agent leaves the reservoir (through open wounds, aerosols, and splatter of body fluids including coughing, sneezing, and saliva)

MODE OF TRANSMISSION
is the way the infectious agent can be passed on (through direct or indirect contact, ingestion, or inhalation)

Fig. 3.1 Break the chain of infection. (Source: Chelsey Armstrong (artist), 2020)

These exposures coupled with less than ideal vaccination rates among both patients and healthcare personnel can result in devastating consequences.

Vaccinations and Immunizations

Vaccinations provide immunization broadly (herd immunity) to not just healthcare personnel but to the public. Since this *Guide* is focused on those practicing occupational health and safety, biological safety, and infectious disease prevention and control in the United States, the focus here will be on what is required and recommended in those settings. If you are using this book outside of North America, please refer to great additional recommendations from the World Health Organization Vaccine Action Coalition.

Immunizations work to protect more than just the vaccinated person but also to prevent transmission of an illness to someone else. This creates what is known as "herd immunity" (Fig. 3.2). When a person is vaccinated, it can prevent the spread to others – the herd – even though they may not have been (or wanted to be) vaccinated. One person has the ability to protect many. This only works though if the many (or the majority) have also been vaccinated.

CDC statistics demonstrate dramatic declines in vaccine-preventable diseases when compared with the pre-vaccine era. Table 3.1 lists the changes in reports and cases and their impact on morbidity.

The importance of the MMR vaccine and its ongoing relevance while working and/or practicing in a healthcare or homecare setting today was covered in the previous chapter. In addition, the CDC recommends the following vaccines for healthcare personnel including hepatitis B, flu, chickenpox, tetanus, diphtheria, pertussis, and meningococcal vaccines (Table 3.2). Many times, vaccines are paired together, for example, MMR, TDAP, and even hepatitis A/B. This kills two (or three) proverbial birds with one stone. CDC's vaccine recommendations for adults working in health care include the following:

To the CDC, healthcare workers are defined to include "physicians, nurses, emergency medical personnel, dental professionals and students, medical and nursing students, laboratory technicians, pharmacists, hospital volunteers, and administrative staff" (CDC 2016). As it pertains to OSHA, this excludes students and volunteers (since they are not paid employees). It does include any employee that is potentially exposed to blood, body fluids, or other potentially infectious material (OPIM) as defined and outlined in Chap. 5.

For OSHA standards, this could include regulated waste haulers, environmental services (EVS) personnel, and sterile processing/central supply personnel to name a few. OPIM can be saliva or urine that is contaminated with blood as is common in dental and long-term care settings or blood products like plasma.

Vaccination recommendations may differ and include more or less depending on geography and facility type. For example, there are research facilities, clinical laboratories, and veterinary institutions across the country that specialize in or are at risk

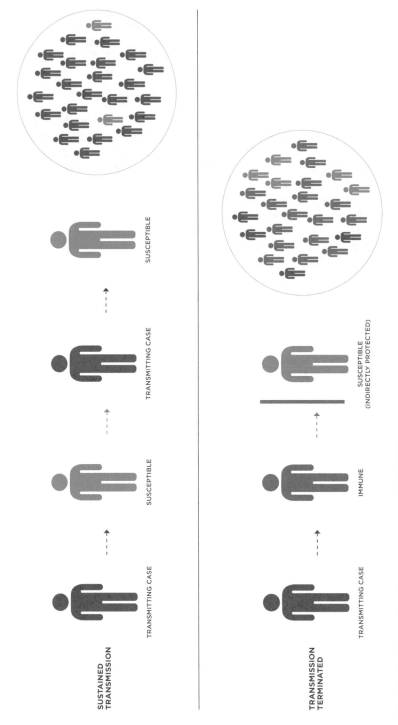

Fig. 3.2 Herd immunity. (Chelsey Armstrong (artist), 2020)

Table 3.1 Vaccines work

Disease	Pre-vaccine era estimated annual morbidity[1,a]	Most recent reports or estimates of US cases[a]	Percent decrease
Diphtheria	21,053	1[2]	>99%
H. influenzae (invasive, <5 years of age)	20,000	33[2,3]	>99%
Hepatitis A	117,333	4000[4]	97%
Hepatitis B (acute)	66,232	20,900[4]	68%
Measles	530,217	273[2]	>99%
Meningococcal disease	2886[5]	340[2]	88%
Mumps	162,344	2251[2]	99%
Pertussis	200,752	13,439[2]	93%
Pneumococcal disease (invasive, <5 years of age)	16,069	1700[6]	89%
Polio (paralytic)	16,316	0[2]	100%
Rotavirus (hospitalizations, <3 years of age)	62,500[7]	30,625[8]	51%
Rubella	47,745	5[2]	>99%
Congenital rubella syndrome	152	0[2]	100%
Smallpox	29,005	0[2]	100%
Tetanus	580	20[2]	97%
Varicella	4,085,120	102,128[9]	98%

Source: IAC 2019

[a]All in chart references are in the References section

Table 3.2 Recommended vaccines for healthcare workers

Vaccines	Recommendations in brief
Hepatitis B	If you don't have documented evidence of a complete hepB vaccine series, or if you don't have an up-to-date blood test that shows you are immune to hepatitis B (i.e., no serologic evidence of immunity or prior vaccination) then you should – Get a 3-dose series of Recombivax HB or Engerix-B (dose #1 now, #2 in 1 month, #3 approximately 5 months after #2) or a 2-dose series of Heplisav-B, with the doses separated by at least 4 weeks – Get an anti-HBs serologic test 1–2 months after the final dose
Flu (influenza)	Get one dose of influenza vaccine annually
MMR (measles, mumps, and rubella)	If you were born in 1957 or later and have not had the MMR vaccine, or if you don't have an up-to-date blood test that shows you are immune to measles or mumps (i.e., no serologic evidence of immunity or prior vaccination), get two doses of MMR (one dose now and the second dose at least 28 days later) If you were born in 1957 or later and have not had the MMR vaccine, or if you don't have an up-to-date blood test that shows you are immune to rubella, only one dose of MMR is recommended. However, you may end up receiving two doses, because the rubella component is in the combination vaccine with measles and mumps For HCWs born before 1957, see the MMR ACIP vaccine recommendations

(continued)

Table 3.2 (continued)

Vaccines	Recommendations in brief
Varicella (chickenpox)	If you have not had chickenpox (varicella), if you haven't had varicella vaccine, or if you don't have an up-to-date blood test that shows you are immune to varicella (i.e., no serologic evidence of immunity or prior vaccination), get two doses of varicella vaccine, 4 weeks apart
Tdap (tetanus, diphtheria, pertussis)	Get a one-time dose of Tdap as soon as possible if you have not received Tdap previously (regardless of when previous dose of Td was received) Get Td boosters every 10 years thereafter Pregnant HCWs need to get a dose of Tdap during each pregnancy
Meningococcal	Those who are routinely exposed to isolates of *N. meningitidis* should get one dose

Source: CDC 2016

of certain pathogens not mentioned above, including human papilloma virus (HPV), yellow fever, rabies, and more. The Advisory Committee on Immunization Practice (ACIP) has many resources available for all vaccination recommendations on their website: https://www.cdc.gov/vaccines/hcp/acip-recs/index.html. They also provide guidance for emergency vaccination programs for diseases like smallpox and avian influenza as well as parameters for prepping, storing, and transporting vaccines.

Tuberculosis (TB)

In addition to the list above, healthcare employers may require annual tuberculin skin testing (TST) for personnel based on risk category (low, medium, high). Tuberculosis (TB) is an infectious disease of global epidemic proportions and in 2008. CDC estimated that approximately one-third of the world population is affected by TB (CDC 2016). TB has also become quite drug resistant and those with underlying infections or illnesses like HIV are more prone to acquiring it.

OSHA has enforcement guidance in place for their compliance safety and health officers (CSHOs) that are conducting inspections in facilities with known or suspected TB (OSHA 2015).

"Emerged" and Emerging Infectious Diseases

SARS-CoV-2 virus that causes COVID-19 has been a lesson learned in the importance of public/private sector collaborations for rapid, safe, and effective vaccine development. This may be an example of how the world has been complacent about the ready availability of vaccines and taken for granted their role in population health. During the 2020 pandemic, it became increasingly clear that there could not be a loosening of social and/or physical distancing, especially for high-risk persons, until a vaccine is available for broad use.

Since a person carrying or infected with COVID-19 may be asymptomatic – either throughout the entirety of infection or in the early stages – they can be shedding the virus to others who may not be able to fight it off. Those with underlying chronic conditions like diabetes and metabolic disorders, heart disease, lung disorders including asthma, autoimmune disorders, and more. This is why physical distancing, wearing masks in public, and frequent handwashing is important in absence of a vaccine, but really whether a vaccine is available or not. To protect those who may not be able to protect themselves. This includes health care, transport, law enforcement, utility, sanitation, and other essential personnel. COVID-19 is considered "emerged" as we have already experienced a devastating global impact. This will also be an important element in future – yet unknown – emerging infectious diseases.

Employee Access to Medical Records

Your role may have responsibility for maintaining current employee vaccination records or receiving records for new hires previously vaccinated. For these responsibilities, it is important to mention that there are standards in place governing employee medical records.

OSHA standard 29 CFR 1910.1020 *Access to employee exposure and medical records* is the most critical of those. Since issues about access and confidentiality – both for the employer and employee – can be complicated, OSHA offers compliance assistance for free by phone 800–321-OSHA and on their website: osha.gov. They also offer a litany of interpretations based on letters and questions that others have written in.

It is important to note that in times of outbreaks, epidemics, and/or pandemics that if employers are conducting employee screening, such as daily temperature-taking, that confidentiality of results must be kept intact. This means that "medical procedures" and recordkeeping should not be done by a facility manager, supervisor, or designated person, rather it should be done by a healthcare practitioner. That practitioner keeps exposure and medical records in a manner that the employer does not have access to records and/or notes that could result in any kind of discrimination to that employee.

Hierarchy of Controls

In Chap. 1, the hierarchy of controls (Fig. 3.3) was introduced. For seasoned industrial hygienists, this is second nature. For those just starting out or moving into occupational health from a different field, a review may be handy.

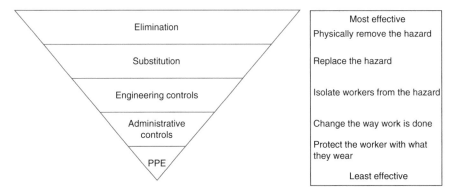

Fig. 3.3 Hierarchy of controls. (Source: NIOSH 2015. Retrieved from https://www.cdc.gov/niosh/topics/hierarchy/default.html)

Elimination

At the top of the hierarchy and the most effective control for preventing occupational illness, injury, or infection is "elimination." This means that hazards are physically removed from a workplace. Since it is difficult to remove an actual patient, as it relates occupational exposure to infectious disease in healthcare, it could mean that instead of having isolation rooms on all hospital floors or in all departments/units, there is only one area for patients in isolation so that the "hazard" – the patient known or suspected to be colonized or infected with a pathogen – is physically "eliminated" from all other departments. It might also mean sending all diagnostic testing to a third-party clinical laboratory, thus removing the hazards associated with infectious disease diagnostics in one facility.

Substitution

Substitution is easier to provide examples with chemical hazards. For example, semi-critical medical devices such as endoscopes used in procedures like colonoscopies are high level disinfected. In years past, glutaraldehyde was regularly used, and it is now substituted with ortho-phthalaldehyde (OPA). OPA is a safer alternative, less toxic, and less of a skin and respiratory system sensitizer.

In health care and as it relates specifically to infectious disease, this may mean substituting an actual blood or body fluids (e.g., urine) used in research facilities with its synthetic counterpart. It may also mean the substitution of a reusable medical device with a disposable product therefore reducing the need altogether for cleaning, disinfecting, or sterilizing it. There are many patient care items, personal protective equipment, and medical devices that are available in disposable versions including blood pressure cuffs, patient and isolation gowns, eye protection, scalpel blades and handles, and more.

Box 3.1

Examples of engineering controls that isolate healthcare personnel from pathogens include:

- High-efficiency particulate air (HEPA) filtration in ventilation systems
- Fume hoods or biological safety cabinets used in clinical labs, research labs, and pharmacies
- Safer medical devices like syringes, blood collection, skin closure, sutures, scalpels, and other devices with built-in safety features isolate the needle or sharp (also known as devices with sharps injury prevetion (SIP) features or "SESIPS" by OSHA)
- Engineered or technical textiles or surfaces worn as uniforms or used for upholstery, patient care items, or environmental surfaces. These can have built in antimicrobial properties
- Closed suction canisters and barrier controls for toilet plume aerosols

Engineering Controls

Engineering controls are designed to isolate people from hazards and should always be considered before PPE (Box 3.1). It's safer to let the building or ventilation or safety-engineered device protect the worker than expecting the worker to protect themselves each and every time.

All of these are designed or engineered to be safer because they filter, kill, denature, contain, block, or isolate microbes and contaminants and have the ability to control hazards better than their non-engineered, "conventional" alternatives. As many of us hope, one day engineering controls in the form of safer devices will become so common place that they will become the new "conventional" device.

Work Practice Controls

While sometimes not explicitly illustrated in the hierarchy of controls, work practice controls are "controls that reduce the likelihood of exposure by altering the manner in which a task is performed (e.g., prohibiting recapping of needles by a two-handed technique)" (OSHA 2001). They include behaviors that the worker must take on as it relates to their selves and their environment. Some examples of work practice controls include:

- Appropriate procedures for hand washing and hand hygiene
- Activation of the safety mechanism on a safer medical or SIP device
- Immediate and safe sharps disposal after device activation and use
- Safe and secure patient specimen handling to the clinical lab
- Handling, transporting, and sortin To be effective, PPE must be avail g laundry safely
- Safe and effective cleaning, disinfection, and/or sterilization of reusable medical devices and surfaces

Work practice controls are documented in the Exposure Control Plan, Exposure or Risk Assessment, and Job Task Analyses. Controls can change over time based on the procedures being performed and the patient population of your facility. Work practices are oftentimes a critical element of engineering controls when engineering controls cannot by themselves eliminate a hazard completely. For example, today many safer medical devices require activation of a safety mechanism, say a button that retracts a needle used for blood collection. While the safer device is the engineering control, it does require a work practice control to more adequately protect the worker – depressing the button.

Administrative Controls

Administrative controls are designed or put in place to change the way people work. They are often incorporated into institutions' cultures and/or climates of safety. They take the form of policies and processes.

Administrative controls can include written safety protocols, scheduling and staffing, supervisory responsibilities, and facility-based policy. In many healthcare facilities, these materialize as elimination of mandatory over-time hours to decrease errors from fatigue, rotating personnel in and out of repetitive tasks such as sterile instrument processing, stretch breaks for those working in sedentary/immobile work stations (desks, cubicles), and decreasing time and exposure for those doing hazardous tasks like radiation or X-ray.

In the case of infectious disease, this could mean the use of nearly any or all of these. For example, in endoscope reprocessing, it may mean rotating personnel that pre-clean or brush endoscopes. This can not only decrease potential exposure time to blood and body fluids but to also decrease the repetitive motion required during this motion intensive step of high-level disinfection.

Simple examples of behaviors that are instituted as administrative policies can include the concepts of "covering your cough" with the inside crook of your elbow or going "bare below the elbow" to prevent cross-contamination and transmission of pathogens via hands, cuffs, or sleeves (Fig. 3.4). These types of controls work to protect worker, patient, and community. While they require an individual to act (work practice control), they are instituted as mandatory protocols within a facility (administrative controls) and are in place by employers to protect workers and their patients.

In the realm of sharps safety or needlestick prevention, this could mean "ditching the pinch" and selecting the right size needle for injecting a subcutaneous medication like insulin or giving a flu vaccine. Ditching the pinch means that the person giving the injection does not grab skin with one hand to give the injection with their dominant hand. This administrative practice becomes policy and has the ability to prevent bilateral sharps injuries (injuries to the other hand or finger) to clinical practitioners (Black 2013).

Fig. 3.4 Cover your cough. (Source: CDC n.d-a. Retrieved from https://www.cdc.gov/flu/pdf/protect/cdc_cough.pdf)

Another example of an administrative control has been championed by National Nurses United and the American Nurses Association in the form of state-based advocacy (legislation) for safe nurse to patient ratios. Adequate staffing saves lives. Safe ratios ultimately result in better care for patients but also provide higher-quality environments for clinicians so that they can take their time and have the ability to critically think through all actions. Healthcare facilities, especially hospitals, are often overcrowded and understaffed. Situations like this can result in rushing and can cause a great deal of stress, increasing the likelihood that corners are forced to be cut, and healthcare workers are put in very taxing positions compromising their safety.

Some argue that training and education are an administrative control because it is designed by default to change the way people work – to make them want to work safer. Several examples above represent administrative controls that rely not just on internal policies being set but work practice controls and training. Some feel that training and education accompany all levels of the hierarchy and not one tier specifically.

Personal Protective Equipment (PPE)

Finally, the least effective control in the hierarchy is PPE or barrier garments. This is the least effective because it is the most subjective. This is covered in more detail in Chap. 9.

To be effective, PPE must be available, accessible, appropriate, donned appropriately, doffed appropriately, and disposed of safely and adequately. If PPE is reusable, it must be containerized and labeled prior to reprocessing safely. Determining whether to use disposable (single use) or reusable PPE should be part of your exposure control and risk assessment plans, keeping in mind not just the user's safety, but all those who may come into contact with it downstream. It must also provide the level of protection that is effective for the biological hazard at hand. Food service gloves are inappropriate for patient care. Surgical masks are inappropriate substitutions for respirators. Isolation gowns that are hazard-specific must be worn correctly so as not to fail to protect the wearers' collar, sleeves, back, etc.

Oftentimes institutions and personnel forget whether PPE is for their benefit – to protect them – or for their patients' benefit, to protect the patient. It is intended to protect the worker, but in many cases, there is double benefit, and both are protected.

One must remember that gloves, for example, must be donned (put on) at the appropriate time. Safe donning and doffing procedures are found in Table 3.3. If gloves are put on too early and doors are open, counters are touched, bedrails are lowered, and then a patient's wound dressing is changed that those gloved hands have now become the vector for whatever pathogens were on those surfaces to the patient's compromised skin. In this case, gloves are neither protecting worker nor patient. PPE must also be disposed of correctly to protect all of those downstream that may come into contact with them, especially environmental surfaces and transport personnel.

There is an overt overreliance on PPE in health care, especially as it relates to infectious disease because it is difficult if not impossible to "engineer out" the patient. In other industries, their work products are physical widgets, parts, machines, building materials, etc. – in health care the work product is the patient or specimen. The science surrounding engineering controls for biological hazards is growing and expanding every day, and employers are required to keep up with these advancements as required by OSHA.

Table 3.3 Donning and doffing personal protective equipment for isolation precautions

Sequence	PPE	Procedure
Donning		
1	Gown	Fully cover torso from neck to knees, arms to end of wrists, and wrap around the back Fasten in back of neck and waist
2	Respirator[a]	Secure ties or elastic bands at middle of head and neck Fit flexible band to nose bridge Fit snug to face and below chin Fit-check respirator
3	Eye protection, faceshield	Place over face and/or eyes and adjust fit
4	Gloves	Extend to cover wrist of isolation gown
Doffing (reverse order before exiting patient or procedure room)		
1	Gloves	Outside of gloves are contaminated If your hands get contaminated during glove removal, immediately wash your hands or use and alcohol-based hand sanitizer Using a gloved hand, grasp the palm area of the other gloved hand, and peel off first glove Hold removed glove in gloved hand Slide fingers of ungloved hand under remaining glove at wrist and peel off second glove over first glove Discard gloves in a waste container. If visibly contaminated with blood (red bag), otherwise regular closed top trash is recommended *Gowns and gloves can be removed in one step by folding and rolling the gown inside out into a bundle. As you are removing the gown, peel gloves off (only touching the inside of the gloves and gown) – dispose of together in a waste container*
2	Eye protection, faceshield	Outside of eye protection (e.g., goggles) or faceshield are contaminated If your hands get contaminated during eye protection or faceshield removal, immediately wash your hands Remove eye protection or faceshield from the back by lifting head band and/or earpieces If the item is reusable, place in designated receptacle for reprocessing. Otherwise discard in waste container
3	Gown	Gown front and sleeves are contaminated If your hands get contaminated during gown removal, immediately wash your hands Unfasten gown ties, taking care that sleeves don't contact your body when reaching for ties Pull gown away from next and shoulders, touching inside of gown only Turn gown inside out Fold or roll into a bundle and discard in a waste container *Skip if removing gloves and gown together in one step*

(continued)

Table 3.3 (continued)

Sequence	PPE	Procedure
4	Respirator	Front of respirator is contaminated. *Do not touch* If your hands get contaminated during respirator removal, immediately wash your hands Grasp bottom ties or elastics, then the ones at the top, and remove without touching the front Discard in a waste container
5	Wash hands	Wash hands with soap and running water. If a sink is not available, use disinfectant-based hand rub, and then wash hands as soon as possible
6	Exit room/ area	It is important to leave contaminated PPE inside the room to not contaminate the door and/or hallway/common areas

Source: CDC n.d-b. Adapted from https://www.cdc.gov/hai/pdfs/ppe/ppe-sequence.pdf
[a]Note: CDC includes "masks" in their guidance for donning and doffing PPE. Since this book is about preventing occupational exposure to infectious disease and masks are not effective for preventing these exposure types, the chart provides information for respirators only

Table 3.4 Application of the hierarchy of controls to an infectious disease threat

Control	Example
Elimination	Keeping sick patients and workers home Removing needles where possible
Substitution	Regional versus general anesthesia Adhesives or alternates for skin closure versus sutures where possible
Engineering control	Negative pressure rooms, HEPA filtration Sharps with injury prevention features
Administrative control	Limiting, dedicating number of staff Robust room processing (cleaning, disinfection) Safe device disposal, instrument processing No/limited visitors Patients stay in cars versus in waiting rooms if possible
PPE	Respirators (N95, PAPR, elastomeric), faceshields, protective eyewear, gowns, double gloving

Hopefully, if you had not heard of or used the hierarchy of controls before, you are now a master of the concept and its application to preventing occupational infectious disease. Some hazards require the pursuit of multiple controls. In a case like a patient with active TB, HEPA filtration, positive pressure, safer medical devices, PPE, and administrative controls including signage will all need to be in place as each control serves to protect environment, worker, patient, and facility.

Table 3.4 shows a matrix for utilization of the hierarchy for an infectious disease threat.

Workers' Rights

It may be most appropriate to mention again that healthcare employers are ultimately responsible for protecting their work force. While there is a great reliance on personnel to take action to protect themselves when other forms of the hierarchy cannot protect thoroughly, it must be in the form of a strong, unwavering institutional policy. Workers' rights are protected by law.

Under federal law, you and your colleagues are entitled to a safe workplace. Your employer must provide a workplace free of known health and safety hazards, and your job is essential to making that happen. If workers have concerns, they have the right to speak up without fear of retaliation.

According to OSHA, you and your staff have the right to:

- Be trained in a language you understand
- Work on machines that are safe
- Be provided required safety gear, such as gloves
- Be protected from toxic chemicals
- Request an OSHA inspection and speak to the inspector
- Report an injury or illness and get copies of your medical records
- See copies of the workplace injury and illness log
- Review records of work-related injuries and illnesses
- Get copies of test results done to find hazards in the workplace (OSHA n.d.)

If any of these elements are not being met and employees ask you about how to contact OSHA and file a complaint, it can be done directly (online, mail, fax, or phone). The OSHA website provides all of the information needed: https://www.osha.gov/workers/index.html.

Not all responsibility falls on the employer. While work practice controls are set as a function of facility administration, leadership, best practice, and a culture of operational safety, it is ultimately the responsibility of each and every employee to adhere to that practice, to be accountable to follow policies, protocols, and practices that are in place to protect themselves, their colleagues, and their patients.

Placing blame on others is sometimes easier than focusing inward on our own behaviors. Ultimately, institutional practices rely on each piece of its parts, each member of its collective body doing what's right, what's safe, and what provides the best outcome. Let us not underplay or overlook the importance of individuals being responsible stewards of safety and well-being.

Tools and Resources
Free Resources for Vaccination and Immunization Programs
- CDC Advisory Committee on Immunization Practice (ACIP) website: https://www.cdc.gov/vaccines/hcp/acip-recs/index.html.
- CDC Current Outbreak List. https://www.cdc.gov/outbreaks/index.html
- CDC Guidelines for Preventing the Transmission of *Mycobacterium tuberculosis* in Health-Care Settings, 2005: https://www.cdc.gov/mmwr/preview/mmwrhtml/rr5417a1.htm?s_cid=rr5417a1_e
- CDC National Influenza Week Materials: https://www.cdc.gov/flu/nivw/materials.htm
- CDC Infectious Diseases. https://www.cdc.gov/oid/index.html

- General Best Practice Guidelines for Immunizations: https://www.cdc.gov/vaccines/hcp/acip-recs/general-recs/index.html
- Immunization of Health-Care Personnel: Recommendations of the Advisory Committee on Immunization Practices (ACIP): https://www.cdc.gov/mmwr/preview/mmwrhtml/rr6007a1.htm
- Immunize.org http://immunize.org/catg.d/p4037.pdf
- OSHA Access to Medical Records Letters of Interpretation https://www.osha.gov/pls/oshaweb/owaquery.query_docs?src_doc_type=INTERPRETATIONS&src_anchor_name=1910.1020&src_ex_doc_type=INTERPRETATIONS&src_unique_file=I19851108B
- OSHA Compliance Directive Enforcement Procedures and Scheduling for Occupational Exposure to Tuberculosis: https://www.osha.gov/OshDoc/Directive_pdf/CPL_02-02-078.pdf
- OSHA Tuberculosis Page: https://www.osha.gov/SLTC/tuberculosis/index.html
- News Updates. Texas Department of State Health Services. https://dshs.texas.gov/news/updates.shtm.
- Vaccines & Immunizations: https://www.cdc.gov/vaccines/index.html
- Worksite Flu Shot Campaigns: http://info.totalwellnesshealth.com/blog/bid/303728/10-Creative-Worksite-Flu-Shot-Program-Campaigns
- World Health Organization Vaccine Action Coalition: http://www.immunize.org/, 2019

Free Sample Campaigns: Administrative Controls
Employee Infection Prevention
- Bare Below the Elbow: (UK National Health System) http://www.icid.salisbury.nhs.uk/ClinicalManagement/operationalissues/Pages/BarebelowelbowUniformPolicies.aspx
- APIC Break the Chain of Infection http://professionals.site.apic.org/protect-your-patients/break-the-chain-of-infection/
- CDC Cover Your Cough https://www.cdc.gov/flu/protect/covercough.htm
- Ditch the Pinch http://www.sciencedirect.com/science/article/pii/S01966553312013727

Employee Health Management Measures and Metrics
- Health Enhancement Research Organization and Population Health Alliance. *Program Measurement and Evaluation Guide: Core Metrics for Employee Health Management.* 2015 http://hero-health.org/wp-content/uploads/2015/02/HERO-PHA-Metrics-Guide-FINAL.pdf

> **Free, All Access Online Training**
> - A Train Continuing Education for Health Professionals Bloodborne Pathogens https://www.atrainceu.com/course-module/1848894-103_bloodborne-pathogens-module-01
> - CDC Immunization Education & Training https://www.cdc.gov/vaccines/ed/index.html
> - CDC Learning Connection https://www.cdc.gov/learning/about/index.html
> - CDC Workplace Health Resource Center https://www.cdc.gov/workplace-healthpromotion/initiatives/resource-center/index.html
> - Health Care Provider Infection Control Training (New York State) https://www.health.ny.gov/professionals/diseases/reporting/communicable/infection/hcp_training.htm

References

Black, L. (2013). Ditch the pinch: Bilateral exposure injuries during subcutaneous injection. *American Journal of Infection Control, 41*(9), 815–819.

CDC. (2016, May). *Recommended vaccines for healthcare workers.* https://www.cdc.gov/vaccines/adults/rec-vac/hcw.html

CDC. (2019). *Vaccines Work!* http://immunize.org/catg.d/p4037.pdf

CDC. JAMA November 14, 2007; 298(18):2155–63.

CDC. National notifiable diseases surveillance system, week 52 (provisional data), weekly tables of infectious disease data, Atlanta, GA. CDC Division of Health Informatics and Surveillance. Available at Accessed 4 Jan 2019. www.cdc.gov/nndss/infectious-tables.html. Accessed 4 Jan 2019.

CDC. Viral Hepatitis Surveillance - United States, 2016.

CDC. MMWR October 6, 1995; 43(53):1–98.

CDC. MMWR, February 6, 2009; 58(RR-2);1–25.

CDC. New Vaccine Surveillance Network, 2017 data (unpublished); U.S. rotavirus disease now has a biennial pattern.

CDC. Varicella Program, 2017 data (unpublished).

CDC. (n.d.a). Cover Your Cough.

CDC. (n.d.b). Sequence for Personal Protective Equipment.

International Safety Center. (2019). *Exposure Prevention Information Network (EPINet) report for blood and body fluid exposures.*

NIOSH. (2015). *Hierarchy of controls.* https://www.cdc.gov/niosh/topics/hierarchy/default.html

OSHA. (2001). 29 CFR 1910.1030 *Bloodborne pathogens standard.* https://www.osha.gov/pls/oshaweb/owadisp.show_document?p_table=standards&p_id=10051

OSHA. (2015). CPL 02-02-078 *Enforcement procedures and scheduling for occupational exposure to tuberculosis.* https://www.osha.gov/OshDoc/Directive_pdf/CPL_02-02-078.pdf

OSHA. (n.d.). *Concerned about health and safety on the job?* https://www.cdc.gov/flu/pdf/protect/cdc_cough.pdf

Chapter 4
Microbiology Basics

Objectives
- Provide a background on microbes most likely to serve as an occupational exposure risk.
- Describe how microorganisms propagate and transmit.
- Describe why some microorganisms cause disease (pathogenic).
- Identify control strategies to mitigate exposure risk.
- Highlight elements of post-exposure prophylaxis and antimicrobial stewardship plans.

Introduction

If you are a professional microbiologist or long-time infection preventionist or even an industrial hygienist that has focused on infectious disease, you can breeze right over this chapter. For those of you starting out or for those who need a booster dose of biology, this chapter is for you! This chapter covers the basics of microbiology, including how pathogens like viruses, bacteria, fungi, protozoans, worms, and spores grow, propagate, travel, and ultimately cause infection and illness in people. Nearly all infection prevention resources that you will find focus on the transmission of microorganisms that can cause healthcare associated infections in patients and while the underlying themes are the same, the practice and impact on workers is different because unlike patients that are admitted and discharged over mostly small windows of time, personnel can be affected by pathogens over decades that span an entire career.

While healthcare personnel are mostly healthy – the likelihood that ongoing exposure to pathogens in the patient care environment will cause a debilitating disease, disability, or death in them is lower than for patients who may be severely immunocompromised. This, however, does not mean that a worker who is exposed

© Springer Nature Switzerland AG 2020
A. H. Mitchell, *Preventing Occupational Exposures to Infectious Disease in Health Care*, https://doi.org/10.1007/978-3-030-56039-3_4

and potentially colonized or ill but not yet experiencing symptoms cannot transfer pathogens on their skin, uniforms, or patient care items (like a stethoscope) home to their families. This could be especially true for a new mom caring for a newborn at home or someone taking care of an elderly parent.

Using the concepts and practices of universal or standard precautions, means assuming that all surfaces in the healthcare environment are potentially contaminated and therefore serve as a potential harbor for pathogens to be spread. These contaminants can cause infection, illness, or disease in any population of people (or animals) that person comes into contact during or after their work shift.

Some microorganisms are so hearty they can live and replicate on porous (uniforms, scrubs, upholstery) and nonporous (countertops, sinks, doorknobs, tablets, and smart phones) surfaces for hours or even days. The makeup and qualities of certain microorganisms make them better at living longer in and on environments where others may not fare as well and die quickly.

To put it simply, pathogens have one job –live long enough to reproduce and cause harm.

They will do this at nearly any cost and over the centuries have adapted well. *Clostridium difficile* (*C. diff*), for example, is so good at its job that it lives one way inside bodies – its vulnerable vegetative state – and an entirely different way in the environment, its hearty endospore state.

C. diff is also quite resilient to most surface cleaners and disinfectants. Since it is spread through stool (diarrhea), it has a medium that is seen and experienced frequently in health care and in large volumes and velocities.

Not only are these organisms smart and adaptive; they have managed to become resistant to our arsenal of antimicrobial drugs and therapies. Since pharmaceutical companies tend to like to develop, commercialize, and sell drugs that people take daily, antibiotics are may not be a high priority for them. As such, research and development for new and innovative antimicrobial treatments falls behind research for more chronic diseases like diabetes, asthma, and high blood pressure.

Our best defense is prevention: prevent exposure to worker, prevent exposure to patient, and outsmart microbes.

Categories of Microorganisms and Disease-Causing Properties

The pathogens and/or categories of pathogens (Fig. 4.1) that are most relevant to health care are:

- *Acinetobacter*
- *Burkholderia cepacia*
- *Candida auris*
- *Clostridium difficile*
- *Clostridium sordellii*
- Coronavirus (SARS-CoV)
- Enterobacteriaceae (carbapenem-resistant)

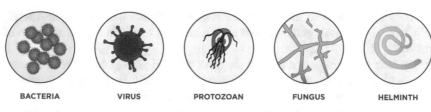

Fig. 4.1 Types of infectious agents. (Chelsey Armstrong (artist), 2020)

- Gram-negative bacteria
- Hepatitis
- Human immunodeficiency virus (HIV/AIDS)
- Influenza
- *Klebsiella*
- Methicillin-resistant *Staphylococcus aureus* (MRSA)
- *Mycobacterium abscessus*
- Mycobacterium tuberculosis – tuberculosis (TB)
- *Neisseria gonorrhoeae*
- Norovirus
- *Pseudomonas aeruginosa*
- *Staphylococcus aureus*
- Vancomycin-intermediate *Staphylococcus aureus* (VISA) and vancomycin-resistant *Staphylococcus aureus* (VRSA)
- Vancomycin-resistant *Enterococci* (VRE)

Most of these pathogens, like bacteria, are cellular living organisms and have the ability to reproduce outside a human or animal host. Bloodborne viruses like HIV are considered "nonliving" or acellular because they need to be safely inside a host to replicate. Whatever the characteristics of the organism itself, all have the potential to pose serious negative effects to patients and workers.

There are additional pathogens that cause occupational illness and disease including anthrax, mostly in veterinary and agricultural settings, and other irritants that can cause pneumonia and lung diseases, but since this resource is dedicated to occupational infectious diseases in health care, focus will not be on those contaminants. It is not, however, meant to underplay their importance and impact.

Transition and Propagation of Pathogenic Microorganisms

In general, microbes are ingenious. This became all too clear during the rapid spread of SAR-CoV-2 around the world in 2019/2020.

Their sole purpose in life is to reproduce and cause harm. Most pathogens are able to survive outside a human or animal host for some amount of time in a vegetative state (living) in a reservoir. A few bacteria can even produce an endospore (*Clostridium* and *Bacillus*), spore (fungi), or a cyst (protozoan like *Cryptosporidium*) which is a dormant body that can "come back to life" once it enters a host. A reservoir might be the soil, water, or even air. All surfaces matter in the transmission of microbes.

Bacteria and viruses are usually the most relevant pathogens in the healthcare setting to both patient and worker (Bennett et al. 2015). However, all pathogens have similar routes of contact transport – direct and indirect.

Direct routes of transmission occur when there is physical contact between an infected (or colonized) person (patient, visitor, family member, or co-worker) and a susceptible person (healthcare worker). This is typically via transfer from contaminated hands to mucous membranes (eyes, nose, mouth) or a compromised area of non-intact skin (open wound, burn, abrasion, etc.).

Indirect transmission occurs when pathogens spread through the air and other mechanisms, for example, contaminated objects (bed rails, eating utensils, curtains), food and drinking water, airborne (tuberculosis), animals, insect bites (Lyme disease), or the environment (cooling towers). For any pathogen to be successful, it must first find a portal of entry in to the host by any one of these transmission routes.

Once a pathogen is transmitted to a susceptible host and gains an entry, the infection process can take place. Pathogens are diabolical adversaries for our immune system. They have a variety of weapons in their arsenal to hide and survive in our bodies so that they can establish an infection and cause illness.

For example, tuberculosis pathogens can survive in one of our primary defense cells – the macrophage. Likewise, HIV can integrate and hide in our helper T cells (CD4) until a later time when they can emerge and kill off our CD4 cells, which make humans very susceptible to other agents of disease.

Pathogens can even mutate to change their camouflage (outer surfaces), secrete a sticky capsule (bacteria) or envelope (viruses) to hide from our immune system. If they are successful, they will create toxins and enzymes that cause damage to our bodies. Eventually they will be able to leave our body through a portal of exit to reestablish themselves in the environment or another host.

The way a pathogen impacts the body could be different person to person. This was observed during the COVID-19 pandemic as people were experiencing a range in devastating symptoms from minor cough and fever, to blood and cardiovascular disorders, manifestations in the gut and skin, and total loss of lung function and oxygen circulation. A pathogen may likely attack the body's weakest system, which is all the more reason to stay diligent about nutrition, exercise, stress reduction, not smoking, and maintaining a healthy weight.

Biofilm

Some bacteria (*Pseudomonas*, *Staphylococcus*, and others) have the ability to create a biofilm on both external (in the environment) and internal (in the body) objects. A biofilm is a sort of "living mesh" of bacterial cells.

One can envision these biofilms as similar to a slime layer on objects composed of many layers of interwoven bacteria with other materials. Strictly defined, a *biofilm* is any group of microorganisms in which cells stick to each other and often also to a surface. These adherent cells become embedded within a slimy matrix that is composed of extracellular polymeric substances (EPS).

This living matrix of bacteria and EPS can be found on medical implants like heart valves and knee/hip replacements. Likewise, they are found in IV tubing, catheters, or needleless access devices, which means a patient can be continuously exposed to bacteria. The biofilm will "break off" of these materials and attack the body.

When a person has a biofilm, it becomes very difficult, if not impossible, to deliver an antibiotic that can penetrate the inner part of the mesh/matrix of bacteria. Thus, one may have to live with the biofilm and be placed on ongoing antimicrobial therapy. Ongoing therapy has a number of negative side effects including developing resistance and tiring organs as they continue to try to process a foreign chemical (drug).

Ultimately, there is an ongoing war of "give and take" in which the host is constantly fighting. In most cases, our bodies are equipped with natural ways (healthy immune systems) to adapt to the weapons that pathogens use against us. However, sometimes the human body needs help in the form of antimicrobial agents (e.g., antibiotics) and vaccines to prevent the infection from ever becoming established in the body.

Protections and Controls

Preventing occupational exposure to microorganisms is more complicated than protecting patients from them – simply because patients are at the mercy of the healthcare facility to do all that it can (Box 4.1).

Box 4.1 Practices for Preventing Healthcare-Associated Infections in Patients
- Making sure indwelling devices are removed as soon as possible
- Conducting rigorous and effective skin disinfection prior to procedures
- Cleaning and disinfecting environmental surfaces and patient care items
- Performing presurgical antimicrobial prophylaxis
- Regulating metabolic diseases like diabetes
- Being diligent about administering fluids via needleless connectors
- Effectively maintaining wounds
- Ensuring that everyone is using proper hand hygiene
- And more

Box 4.2 Active Controls for Occupations in Health Care
- Respiratory protection programs, including fit testing
- Vaccination and immunization programs
- Engineering control use, including safety-engineered medical devices to prevent sharps injuries
- PPE use, compliance, and ready accessibility

  - Eye protection, including protective eyewear, goggles, and faceshields
  - Face protection for inhalation, including respirators
  - Body protection, barrier garments, including gowns
  - Gloves, including double gloving for surgery and material types (latex, nitrile, vinyl)

- Work practice controls, including proper donning/doffing of PPE and sharps/medical waste disposal and transport
- Administrative controls, such as staying home when ill, adequate staffing, effective waste management, and specimen transport
- Proper hygiene, including handwashing, bathing, and personal laundry
- Adequate, safe, and effective laundering
- Surface cleaning and disinfection
- Instrument and device cleaning and disinfection
- Training, education, and hazard communication including not just annual training but creation of ongoing campaigns, as well as biohazard and infectious labeling and signage

As it relates to occupational controls, workers take an active role in their own prevention in addition to the "passive" and ongoing institutional controls that are put in place to protect them like HEPA filtration, adequate room air exchanges, safe water, mold remediation programs during construction, and environmental surface safety (Box 4.2).

Ultimately it is paramount to build comprehensive programs in your facility that incorporate all controls necessary to prevent occupational exposure to infectious disease. The real benefit here – other than preventing illness, disability, and death among workers – is the synergistic effects that these controls have on protecting patients and communities. In essence, these controls serve the public's health.

Post-exposure Prophylaxis and Antimicrobial Stewardship

When someone becomes infected and the disease process could be underway, what is the first step? Post-exposure prophylaxis and drug therapy are the primary response in most instances. A treatment administered following exposure to a pathogen which attempts to block or reduce injury or infection is referred to as post-exposure prophylaxis. Prophylaxis is a defense or protection.

In some cases, pre-exposure prophylaxis (presurgical antibiotics, vaccines, and immunization) are used as tools to prevent a pathogen from gaining a foothold if they are introduced. Those traveling to countries or regions with high rates of malaria, for instance, take an antimalarial medication to help prevent the infection from occurring.

Post-exposure prophylaxis (PEP), on the other hand, might concern the treatment of a healthcare worker exposed by a needlestick to HIV. PEP (depending on the results of source testing) may include drug therapy such as AZT to prevent the HIV virus from infecting its new host.

Of primary concern with any drug therapy or protocol for treatment is the necessity to identify the pathogen correctly. Credentialed medical (clinical) laboratory professionals conduct pathogen identification. They are responsible for identifying the pathogen (bacteria, virus, fungus, etc.) so that the proper antibiotics or antimicrobials can be prescribed as quickly as possible.

Remember, pathogens are ingenious and diabolical. They are ingenious enough to mutate rapidly when the wrong drug or the wrong dose is given.

Pathogens use "survival of the fittest" to mutate (change their genetic makeup) in the presence of antimicrobial agents (antibiotics, antivirals, antifungals, etc.). It is our professional responsibility to limit this from happening. Antimicrobial stewardship programs are now becoming part of the healthcare landscape at all levels.

There are training modules available to use for all different levels of knowledge and understanding, including some basic versions that are free, but many are available for a fee (Box 4.3).

Box 4.3 Training Session/Educational Design Outline
- Quizlet Flashcards for Infection Control. https://quizlet.com/206207802/quiz-1-infection-control-flash-cards/
- Quizlet for Microbiology. https://quizlet.com/subject/microbiology/
- APIC CIC Exam Study Guide* http://apic.org/Resource_/ProductDownloadItemForm/be07cfe8-08bf-4cde-8b63-06d6e9c79040/File/Study%20Guide%20Preview.pdf
- ASM's Image Gallery, Laboratory Protocols, Curriculum Archive, and Visual Media Briefs: http://www.asmscience.org/VisualLibrary
- CDC Antibiotics Quiz. https://www.cdc.gov/antibiotic-use/community/about/quiz.html
- Online HCAI / IPC / AMR / AMS / Training Resources from Reflections in Infection Prevention and Control (to share with infection prevention and control) https://reflectionsipc.com/2017/12/14/online-hcai-ipc-amr-ams-training-resources/#more-3837

*Note: Unfortunately, Certified Infection Control practitioners are only asked about 10 questions {~5%} on occupational/employee health which does highlight the need for a resource like this. Exam Outline: https://www.cbic.org/certification/examination-content-outline

Tools and Resources: Free, All Access
- CDC. *Diseases and Organisms in Healthcare Settings.* https://www.cdc. gov/hai/organisms/organisms.html
- Mayo Clinic. *Germs: Understand and Protect Against Bacteria, Viruses, and Infection* http://www.mayoclinic.org/diseases-conditions/infectious-diseases/in-depth/germs/ART-20045289
- OSHA. *Infectious Diseases in Healthcare Resource List.* https://www. osha.gov/SLTC/healthcarefacilities/infectious_diseases.html
- American Society for Microbiology Resource Library www.asmscience. org/VisualLibrary

Useful Microbiology Reference Articles

Bergey, D. H., & Holt, J. G. (2000). *Bergey's manual of determinative bacteriology* (9th ed.). Philadelphia: Lippincott Williams & Wilkins.

Caroll, K. C., & Pfaller, M. A. (2019). *Manual of clinical microbiology* (12th ed.). Washington, D.C.: ASM Press.

Rohde, R. E. Two laboratory tests you must demand – advice from MRSA survivors and a scientist. Infection Control.tips http://infectioncontrol.tips/2016/01/11/2la btests-mrsa/

Rohde, R.E. (2014, February 11). The Hidden Profession that Saves Lives – Medical Laboratory Science (also called Clinical Laboratory Science) is one of the most under-recognized health professions – with excellent job prospects. *Elsevier Connect.*   http://www.elsevier.com/connect/ the-hidden-profession-that-saves-lives

Acknowledgments This chapter was co-written with input and contribution by Rodney E. Rohde, PhD, MS, SM(ASCP)[CM], SV[CM], MB[CM], FACSc. Texas State University, College of Health Professions, CLS Program.

Reference

Bennett, J., Dolin, R., & Blaser, M. (2015). *Principles and practice of infectious diseases* (8th ed.). Philadelphia: Elsevier-Saunders.

Chapter 5
Occupational Safety and Health Administration (OSHA) Regulatory Compliance

Objectives
- Provide in-depth information on the elements of OSHA standards applicable to infectious disease in health care
- Describe essential components for compliance with OSHA standards
- Describe importance of compliance with OSHA standards as it relates to citations and fines

Occupational Safety and Health Administration (OSHA)

The Occupational Safety and Health Administration (OSHA) sits within the US Department of Labor and develops, implements, and enforces safety and health standards (regulations) for employers and their employees in all 50 states and US territories. OSHA standards are not recommendations or guidelines; rather, they are enforceable by law. About half of the states in the United States fall under the jurisdiction of Federal OSHA, and the others have their own OSHA "State Plans" with standards that must be "at least as effective as" Federal OSHA standards.

While other regulatory agencies have authority to set standards for infectious disease and the provision of health care from a public health, patient, and consumer safety point of view, OSHA is currently the only agency with regulatory authority to dictate what is required to prevent workplace *occupational exposure to infectious disease*. However, OSHA standards are not meant to be overly prescriptive. Healthcare employers are required to conduct hazard or exposure assessments in order to identify how to best implement controls that eliminate or minimize exposures to the lowest feasible extent. (Note: at the time of writing this book, OSHA does not have a specific infectious disease standard in place; therefore, compliance related to occupational exposures to infectious disease is gleaned from other standards and the General Duty Clause. California OSHA State Plan does have an

© Springer Nature Switzerland AG 2020

A. H. Mitchell, *Preventing Occupational Exposures to Infectious Disease in Health Care*, https://doi.org/10.1007/978-3-030-56039-3_5

Box 5.1 Some Applicable OSHA Standards for Health Care
- Bloodborne Pathogens Standard (29 CFR 1910.1030)
- Personal Protective Equipment (29 CFR 1910.132)
- Eye and Face Protection (29 CFR 1910.133)
- Respiratory Protection Standard (29 CFR 1910.134)
- Hazard Communication (29 CFR 1910.1200)
- Recording and Reporting Occupational Injuries and Illnesses (29 CFR 1904)
- General Duty Clause (OSH Act, 5(a)1)
- CalOSHA Aerosol Transmissible Disease Standard (for those in California only)

Aerosol Transmissible Disease Standard and it is expected that other State Plan States will follow suit.)

Assessments include identification and documentation of job tasks within all professional/personnel categories where either a practice, procedure, duty, or responsibility may result in an exposure risk. Assessments then result in identifying how to determine most effective controls for preventing and mitigating those risks.

Many OSHA standards are written for physical or chemical risks that are easy to see and identify. For example, they include falling and tripping hazards, electrical and fire, exit signs, combustibles, asbestos, confined space, and more.

Microorganisms are present in healthcare environments by the tens of millions, even billions. Resistance and biological uptake is ever changing. They are not visible to the naked eye. For these reasons and more, it is more difficult to develop and promulgate a prescriptive standard taking all factors into account.

As such, where OSHA does not have a hazard-specific standard – in this case for "Infectious Diseases" – OSHA has several standards in place that need to be incorporated into an occupational infectious disease plan that together provide the foundation for safety (Box 5.1).

Bloodborne Pathogens Standard

When thinking about the pathogens that cause infectious disease, most infection preventionists think bacteria like *Mycobacterium* tuberculosis (TB) or viruses like influenza. Relative to OSHA, however, it is the bloodborne pathogens that cause the greatest potential illness or infection risk. The reasoning behind this has a great deal to do with the occupational transmission of the HIV virus, which can result in AIDS, in the early to mid-1980s.

Given the rise in prevalence of HBV, HCV, and HIV (as well as co-infections with one or more) around the world and increasing access of global citizens to US health care, the occupational risks associated with exposure to bloodborne pathogens may be more relevant now than ever.

The Bloodborne Pathogens Standard (BPS) is very comprehensive and includes a great deal of detail. Since most of the elements of the standard are covered in subsequent chapters, this overview chapter provides brief background and information. Consider it your "cut and carry" chapter if you need to develop or design general content for a presentation or training.

The major categories of OSHA BPS requirements include the following (OSHA 2001):

- Exposure control and exposure control plan
- Methods of compliance
- Engineering and work practice controls
- Personal protective equipment
- Regulated waste
- HIV and HBV research laboratories and production facilities
- Hepatitis B vaccination and post-exposure evaluation and follow-up
- Communication of hazards to employees
- Labels and signs
- Information and training
- Recordkeeping
- Sharps Injury Log

Many of these elements are covered in more detail in later chapters. This serves as a high-level description to establish a solid foundation of understanding. There also is a model Exposure Control Plan in Appendix B that can be adapted to any workplace.

Exposure Control and Exposure Control Plan

This section of the standard is mission control. Not only is a facility exposure determination documented here – including all job classifications, duties, tasks, processes, and procedures where there is potential employee exposure to blood, body fluids, or other potentially infectious materials (OPIM) – but also what controls are in place to prevent them, references to safety or infection prevention and control committee minutes, evaluation of safety devices, scheduling grids for training plans, and more.

This is a living, breathing document, and it is the first document (after the Sharps Injury Log) that an OSHA Compliance Safety and Health Officer (CSHO) will ask for during an inspection. The best recommendation is to keep this in a three-ring binder, available as broadly as possible, so that elements can be added, updated, and pulled out for copying/scanning/emailing. The exposure control plan (ECP) is required to be updated annually, so this helps make changes and edits easier.

For example, if the emergency department just evaluated new safety disposable scalpels and documentation of the frontline employee feedback was shared during last month's infection control committee, the minutes of that meeting can be three-ring punched and included in the ECP binder under the "Engineering Controls" tab. Those meeting minutes can be shared with materials management to direct their purchasing and supply chain. Device evaluation forms from TDICT Project can be referenced in the plan (https://tdict.org/tools/medical-device-evaluation-forms/).

There is no requirement that the ECP has to be paper-based, but it does need to be easily accessible to all employees that need it. If it is computer-based, there needs to be clear instructions to any employee with potential exposure to blood or other potentially infectious materials about how and where to access it. If there is a central version of the ECP maintained in a locked office and there is no widespread access to it, this could likely result in a citation should there be an OSHA inspection. Best advice is to really focus here because again, it will be one of the first things an OSHA official will ask for either during an inspection or if exploring consultation services.

Methods of Compliance

Standard precautions should always be followed. Assuming that all blood and body fluids are potentially contaminated with one or many bloodborne pathogens is the most important guiding beacon of practice. Following methods of compliance, including strict adherence to the industrial hygiene hierarchy of controls, is the most comprehensive and effective way to prevent exposures. The hierarchy was covered in detail in Chap. 3 and you can refer back to it if you need to.

Some methods include:

Engineering Controls Engineering controls including what OSHA calls "sharps with engineered sharps injury protections" or "SESIPs" (OSHA 2001). A more commonly used term is "safety-engineered device" or "safer medical device." These include syringes, IV catheters, sutures, blades, or any other needle or sharp with a feature that retracts, sheaths, blunts, or otherwise protects the user from a percutaneous injury.

According to the International Safety Center Exposure Prevention Information Network (EPINet®) data, disposable hypodermic syringes are the devices causing the most needlestick injuries among nurses and sutures the most for physicians (EPINet 2019). Using comparison or benchmark data like that from EPINet or the Massachusetts Department of Public Health Sharps Injury Surveillance System can be good to use as guides for where to begin selecting safety devices in your facility, but nothing is better than using your own Sharps Injury Log data to drive evaluation and selection in your facility.

The best benchmark is zero. Steer clear of using just ratios or rates to guide where you focus. They can however be useful marking your successes or failures over a time period or comparing year to year. Methods of measurement will be covered in detail in Chap. 8.

Work Practice Controls Another control that goes hand in hand with the use of engineering controls is work practice. It is not enough to have a safety device in hand; the safety feature has to be activated – protecting not only device user but all those who come into contact with it throughout its life (environmental services, waste haulers, facilities, laundry, etc.). Another critical work practice is immediate disposal of used, contaminated devices into a sharps container.

EPINet data tells us that of all injuries occurring, more than half of all injuries occurring from safety devices occur because the safety feature or mechanism was not activated (EPINet 2019). This impacts about one-quarter of nonusers or those downstream that experience a sharps injury. Downstream injuries can be devastating for many reasons. First, if a worker sorting laundry is injured because a needle was left in patient bedding, it may be impossible to identify the source patient that device was used on. This means that person may have to undergo rigorous postexposure follow-up and care because it was not known if the patient had a bloodborne disease or not. We owe it to colleagues and co-workers to keep them safe from unknown, unanticipated hazards.

Personal Protective Equipment Personal protective equipment (PPE) including gloves, gowns, eye protection, faceshields, and respirators serve as a means of protection when all other controls in the hierarchy fail to prevent an exposure. The selection, placement, accessibility, use, and compliance with PPE will be covered in depth in Chap. 10.

When thinking about the role of PPE, many lose sight of its purpose. Gloves, for example, are worn in health care to protect both worker from patient and patient from worker. Appropriate timing for donning and doffing can be more critically important than glove use itself for one key reason – gloves like any other surface in health care can be a source of microbial transmission.

From a patient's point of view – if a nurse puts gloves on too soon before performing a patient care task – like changing a wound dressing – the gloves may pick up environmental contaminants along the way from the countertop, bedrail, linen, or privacy curtain prior to touching the patient's skin. This is likely to result in pathogenic transfer from surface to wound potentially resulting in a catastrophic infection.

From a worker's point of view – if this same pair of gloves is not removed at the appropriate time, they become a source of exposure to the nurse. He may inadvertently touch his scrubs or gown or adjust his glasses or eye protection. Since microbes especially more hearty bacteria live comfortably on soft surfaces like textiles or woven materials for hours, the gloves have now served as a vector for transmission of an occupational pathogen.

Regulated Waste Protecting oneself during direct interaction with a patient is an important step in preventing occupational exposure to infectious disease. This is by far an essential element in overall occupational infectious disease and infection prevention. Perhaps this is most crucial to direct care clinical providers like physicians, physician assistants, nurses, nursing assistants, diagnostic imaging technicians, medical technologists, phlebotomists, and other practitioners.

It is in the protection of those downstream that the importance of properly containerizing, color-coding, and labeling regulated waste comes in to play. Clinicians have the benefit of instituting standard precautions when caring for patients and human specimens at the bedside or care site, non-clinicians are not afforded this level of precaution, so they must rely on the provision of a physical barrier to protect them from a bloodborne hazard.

The OSHA BPS has requirements in place for sharps containers and collectors, red or biohazard bags, labels, transport, and more. These sections of the standard provide controls for bloodborne hazards throughout the lifetime of their infective life span. More than a quarter of all contaminated sharps injuries occur to those downstream. It is with the provisions in this section of the standard that preventive measures are addressed.

HIV and HBV Research Laboratories and Production Facilities

Since this *Practical Guide* covers occupational exposure to infectious disease in healthcare settings, it will not provide detailed insights into the regulations for labs that research, develop, and produce bloodborne pathogens and their affiliated products/byproducts. Standard microbiological approaches should be taken, and there are many resources written for those settings, some of which you will find in Chap. 4.

Hepatitis B Vaccination

The hepatitis B virus (HBV) vaccine has been required to be offered by employers in health care since the standard was first released in 1992. At the time, HBV vaccines were not mandatory for children entering school in the United States and served as one of the most important contributions of occupational public health – decreasing incidence of occupational liver cancer. There are many vaccine public health success stories, too many to name, but few have had such a positive influence on cancer – this and the human papilloma virus (HPV) vaccine and subsequent cervical cancer.

The BPS requires that employers offer and pay for the HBV vaccine for all employees with potential occupational exposure to blood and other potentially infectious materials (OPIM). OPIM is a catch-all term that includes body fluids that have the potential to transmit a bloodborne pathogen. While saliva and urine may not be considered OPIM, it is likely in healthcare and/or patient care settings that they are also contaminated with blood. For example, saliva is highly likely to contain bloow in dentistry and during dental procedures or urine is highly likely to contain blood during catheterization. Of note, saliva and sputum can transmit infectious viruses like SARS-CoV-2, but again since OSHA does not (upon writing this book) have a specific infectious disease standard, we are addressing bloodborne pathogens here. There are provisions in the standard if an employee chooses to decline the vaccine and what documentation and protections are then needed as well as parameters for employees who have had the vaccine previously. There is a declination form as part of the Exposure Control Plan in Appendix B.

Given that most professionals entering health care were vaccinated as children since the standard was originally published, it is likely that if OSHA does not provide updated guidance that it will defer as it often does to a sister agency with expertise in the field. In this case, the Centers for Disease Control and Prevention (CDC) and the National Vaccine Advisory Committee (NVAC) have recommendations for vaccinations which are available in Chap. 2.

Post-exposure Evaluation and Follow-up

When an occupational exposure to blood or body fluids occurs, OSHA provides general guidance in the standard itself and defers its practical, clinical guidance to the CDC. Essentially every exposure or injury is going to be different and follow-up dependent on each person, but ultimately the most important first steps are source (patient, specimen) testing (if known) and baseline blood testing for the employee (if source is positive for a bloodborne pathogen). Again, this can be difficult if a needlestick or sharps injury occurs to a worker downstream where the origin of that device is not known.

Since OSHA is in the business of preventing occupational exposures and not in the business of providing clinical guidance, CDC and others, especially the University of California San Francisco (USCF) Post-Exposure Prophylaxis (PEP) Help Line, provide valuable resources for occupational, employee, infectious disease, and emergency health practitioners. More information is available in the Exposure Control Plan in Appendix B.

If you have responsibility for coordinating efforts either for or between the designated professionals that provide post-exposure and employees, make sure you (and they) have the most up-to-date information possible. If an exposure or injury occurs during night shift or weekends when the employee health office is closed, it is vital to set up emergency services, policies, and protocols so that employees, their managers, and facility leadership know exactly what to do, where to go, and how to follow up. Timeliness is of the essence when an exposure occurs. Having a plan in place that is well communicated to everyone is the only way to avoid unnecessary health, psychological, and emotional stress.

CDC provides guidance for potential exposure to HIV, as one example. Process includes the following steps employees need to know (CDC n.d.):

- Know your facility's procedure for reporting an exposure and get evaluated.
- Depending on your evaluation, follow the steps for post-exposure prophylaxis.
- Follow up with your occupational health and/or medical provider during your treatment.
- Perform follow-up testing, if applicable.

Fig. 5.1 The biohazard
symbol. (Source: OSHA
29 CFR 1910.1030)

Communication of Hazards to Employees

Just as students learn differently, intaking and uptaking information in different ways, using different media, so do employees. It's not just that adults learn differently (though they do), it's also that hazards come at them in different ways; physical, liquid, sharp, wet, soft, hard, aerosolized, aerated, and even gaseous. This section of the standard covers mandates for labels and signs, training and education, and written materials.

Labels and Signs

The requirements established in these paragraphs of the OSHA BPS address controls to alert employees to bloodborne hazards. It includes biohazard labels and signs, both black and white and color-coded (Fig. 5.1).

Labels and signs need to be used on sharps containers and collectors, specimen containers, "red bags," contaminated linen bags or receptacles, and potentially infectious materials like therapeutics derived from infectious pathogens (blood, blood components, blood products).

In a laboratory setting, since it is more likely a specimen, blood, or sample will be potentially infectious, not only do these labels need to be prominently placed, there also need to be information about:

- *Name of the infectious agent*
- *Special requirements for entering the area (if applicable)*
- *Name and telephone number of the laboratory director (or other responsible person)*

Information and Training

Employee training is required to be performed both at initial hire and annually thereafter (within 1 year of previous training). The minimum required OSHA BPS curriculum includes the following (OSHA 2001):

- An accessible copy of the regulatory text of the OSHA BPS and an explanation of its contents
- A general explanation of the epidemiology and symptoms of bloodborne diseases
- An explanation of the modes of transmission of bloodborne pathogens
- An explanation of the employer's ECP and ways the employee can obtain a copy of the written plan
- An explanation of the appropriate methods for recognizing tasks and other activities that may involve exposure to blood and other potentially infectious materials
- An explanation of the use and limitations of methods that will prevent or reduce exposure including appropriate engineering controls, work practices, and personal protective equipment
- Information on the types, proper use, location, removal, handling, and decontamination and disposal of personal protective equipment
- An explanation of the basis for selection of PPE
- Information on the HBV vaccine, including information on its efficacy, safety, method of administration, the benefits of being vaccinated, and that the vaccine and vaccination will be offered free of charge
- Information on the appropriate actions to take and persons to contact in an emergency involving blood or OPIM
- An explanation of the procedure to follow if an exposure incident occurs, including the method of reporting the incident and the medical follow-up that will be made available
- Information on the post-exposure evaluation and follow-up that the employer is required to provide for the employee following an exposure incident
- An explanation of the signs and labels and/or color-coding
- An opportunity for *interactive* real-time questions and answers with the person conducting the training session

Not all of the list above needs to be included in the annual and ongoing training for long-time employees. OSHA expects that refresher information is covered if needed but also that content on new processes, procedures, policies, and devices takes up the bulk of the material. In fact, conducting the same training material year after year may result in complacency and boredom. It can result in apathy toward risk ultimately creating an environment where an exposure incident is more likely.

Recordkeeping

Employers are required to keep records for many types of events: training, exposure incident records (Sharps Injury Log), as well as employee medical records (post-exposure, vaccination, etc.).

To note, there are specific requirements to maintain confidentiality of employee medical records that are established through the *Access to employee exposure and medical records* Standard (1910.1020).

Box 5.2 Required Elements of Sharps Injury Log
- The type and brand of device involved in the incident
- The department or work area where the exposure incident occurred
- An explanation of how the incident occurred

(Source: OSHA 2001)

Training records must include the following information:

- The dates of the training sessions
- The contents or a summary of the training sessions
- The names and qualifications of persons conducting the training
- The names and job titles of all persons attending the training sessions

The recordkeeping requirement set forth in the OSHA BPS is unique to any other OSHA standard in that the Needlestick Safety and Prevention Act (Public Law 106-430, 2000) dictated that the BPS include a specific recordkeeping requirement for sharps injuries. The Sharps Injury Log is kept as part of the overall OSHA Injury and Illness Recordkeeping Log (OSHA 300, 300A), but it must include the following information about each contaminated needlestick or sharps injury (Box 5.2):

Personal Protective Equipment and Eye and Face Protection

OSHA's PPE (29 CFR 1910.132) and Eye and Face Protection Standards (29 CFR 1910.133), in a general sense, apply mostly to noninfectious, nonbiological hazards rather than to physical, chemical, or radiologic hazards. The standard has been interpreted by the agency (especially during the COVID-19 pandemic) to apply to infectious disease hazards. The standard bears important mention here because part of keeping microbiological risks at bay is done using cleaners, detergents, disinfectants, antimicrobials, sporicidals, and sterilants. These chemicals are used on hard and soft surfaces, laundry, hands, medical devices, patient care items, and equipment.

One of the most crucial considerations with respect to both personnel and patient safety is the use of chemical and physical hazards in sterile processing departments (SPD) or central sterile supply departments (CSSD). This department in any healthcare facility is the busiest hub. Reusable devices, surgical equipment, and even patient care items like wheelchairs and infusion pumps come in grossly contaminated and are cleaned, disinfected or sterilized, cataloged, stored, and returned to the floors when needed.

SPDs are hot, wet, slippery, cramped, over-crowded, and often understaffed. Biological threats loom here in every microscopic nook and cranny and because devices and equipment are processed using physical cleaning with brushes, pressurized water, steam, chemical disinfectants, and sterilants like hydrogen peroxide and ethylene oxide, the general PPE standard has the greatest degree of application. Many different physical and chemical hazards can potentially harm sterile processing personnel during their job duties.

It covers requirements for supplying and payment of PPE (including eye and face protection), safe design and construction, appropriate donning and doffing procedures, cleaning, and training. This will be covered more in depth in Chap. 10.

Respiratory Protection Standard

In general, the OSHA Respiratory Protection Standard (RPS) (29 CFR 1910.134) can apply to bloodborne pathogens because these are considered splashes and splatters with a physical hazard: blood or body fluids that can result in an exposure to a pathogenic microorganism (OSHA 2011b). The RPS also applies to infectious diseases including tuberculosis, influenza, Ebola virus, as well as procedures during which pathogens could be aerosolized or aerated, for example, when surgical smoke is generated or during surgeries or autopsies of a patient with a known infectious disease.

NOTE: Surgical masks are not respirators and are not technically considered PPE. If a surgical mask is worn in combination with a faceshield; only the faceshield is considered PPE. As it relates to protection of healthcare workers during an infectious disease pandemic like COVID-19, N95s or elastomeric respirators are considered ideal for treating patients with known or suspected disease and/or SARS-CoV-2 exposure.

Respirators include the following types that will be covered in more detail in Chap. 10, and protections in place for COVID-19 will be covered in more detail in Chap. 11:

- Particulate filtering facepiece (e.g., N95, P99, P100)
- Powered air-purifying respirator (PAPR) and elastomeric
- Supplied-air respirator (SAR) or airline respirator
- Self-contained breathing apparatus (SCBA)

Respirators must be NIOSH-certified and worn in accordance with the conditions of that certification (NIOSH 2020). As stated above for PPE, this standard also covers requirements for selection, appropriate selection factors, donning, and doffing, and unique to the RPS is the requirement for respirator fit testing which will be covered later in this *Practical Guide.*

Hazard Communication

As mentioned above, oftentimes occupational exposures to infectious disease occur hand in hand with exposures to hazardous chemicals. The OSHA Hazard Communication "Haz Com" Standard (29 CFR 1910.1200) applies to occupational exposures to hazardous chemicals, including disinfectants, sterilants, specimen fixatives, hazardous drugs, and cleaners often used in healthcare settings (OSHA 2013). It is aptly named and has application for the communication of hazards to employees, including information imparted by the safety data sheets (SDSs) (formerly known as "material safety data sheets" or "MSDSs") that need to accompany chemicals used in a workplace.

Some common hazardous chemicals used for killing infectious microorganisms include chlorine bleach, glutaraldehyde ("glute"), ortho-phthalaldehyde (OPA), formalin, formaldehyde, hydrogen peroxide, and ethylene oxide to name a very few. The Haz Com standard is not specific to cleaners and disinfectants used in health care; rather it generally applies to all hazardous chemicals.

Similar to the OSHA BPS, the Haz Com standard requires making and maintaining a written hazard communication plan. The written plan needs to include not just where and how employees access information about the chemicals but also what precautionary measures to take immediately following an exposure to one. The standard also includes information for labeling, signage, and training.

An SDS needs to include certain information (Box 5.3), and typically these will come directly from the chemical manufacturer, distributor, shipper, or all three. SDSs must be kept in a location where employees and their managers can readily access them during all shifts. A sample SDS is available in Appendix C.

Of note, when using surface disinfectants in healthcare or patient care settings, carefully identify the appropriate disinfectant for the surface being disinfected. What characteristics might the surface have that are unique; these would be different for wood, laminated surfaces, metal, stone, or textiles. It is also important to carefully follow the instructions for use (IFUs) for information on contact time, application, and potential occupational hazards including whether the product can be a skin sensitizer or irritant or a pulmonary irritant. This would then dictate what PPE may be required when using it. It is best to stay away from spray applications as aeration of chemicals can result in asthma or may impact the instrumentation in the room.

Box 5.3 Required Information on a Safety Data Sheet (SDS)
- Chemical identification
- Hazard(s) identification
- Composition/information on ingredients
- First-aid measures
- Fire-fighting measures
- Accidental release measures
- Handling and storage
- Exposure controls/personal protection
- Physical and chemical properties
- Stability and reactivity
- Toxicological information

Source: OSHA Hazard Communication (2013): "Haz Com" Standard (29 CFR 1910.1200)

Recording and Reporting Occupational Injuries and Illnesses

Keeping track of employee injuries and illnesses is not only a useful tool for monitoring the wellness of employees and identifying ways to prevent future exposures, but it is also required by law. The OSHA Recordkeeping Rule (29 CFR 1904) sets forth the required parameters for documenting exposure incidents that can result in occupational illness or infection (OSHA 2020).

As it pertains to occupational infectious disease, some possible exposures resulting in illness can include work-related tuberculosis, influenza, or hepatitis. As we know now, there are documented occupational cases of globally emerging infectious disease including Ebola, Zika, and MERS. At times work-relatedness can be difficult to establish for infectious diseases because they can be prevalent in communities or at home. This is especially true for something with wide spread community exposure and transmission like COVID-19. See Appendix A for all forms and logs required by the Recordkeeping Standard.

Encouraging staff to report injuries and exposures is not only the right thing to do for OSHA compliance, but also having a culture of safety in place that promotes openness and transparency as a means to correct, improve, and grow is critical. It can serve as a means to recruit staff locally, even to retain employees since health care is a competitive employer, especially in urban and suburban areas. It may even be a way to recruit patients and community projects locally as a steward of doing what's right, fair, and safe.

Work-relatedness can be established using the following decision-making criteria (Fig. 5.2):

Fig. 5.2 Determining work-relatedness and recordkeeping

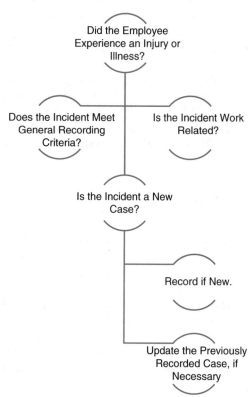

Other OSHA Standards and Resources

In addition to the specific OSHA standards mentioned in this chapter, the agency also provides a bounty of resources, documents, electronic tools (e-Tools), tricks of the trade, compliance assistance guidance, booklets, and so many other valuable tools through their website (www.osha.gov). OSHA also offers free on-site consultation assistance for facilities of all sizes. Do not be afraid to take advantage of this wonderful service. To find a service in your area, log on to https://www.osha.gov/dcsp/smallbusiness/consult.html.

One tool that is quite useful in building an overall healthcare occupational safety and health program (beyond just bloodborne and infectious disease) is the Hospital e-Tool available online at https://www.osha.gov/SLTC/etools/hospital/. This also has a Long Term Care Nursing Home version.

A note on OSHA inspections:

- If you find yourself being inspected by OSHA, know that they will ask for your written program plans and injury/illness logs as one of the first orders of business. Do yourself, your facility, and your employees a favor, and keep these important written plans and records current and accessible. The resources in this *Practical Guide* are designed to help you stay on top of what is required and important to protect personnel from infectious disease.
- Do not think that just because there is not a specific "Infectious Disease" OSHA standard that they will not enforce or even cite your facility for knowing about a hazard and not doing anything about it. In these situations, OSHA exercises its regulatory muscles by using what is called the General Duty Clause of the OSH Act – or "5(a)(1)."
- Citations under 5(a)(1) are issued when an employer fails to furnish each employee "a place of employment free from recognized hazards." Since California is currently the only state with an Aerosol Transmissible Disease Standard (Title 8 CCR §5199) that addresses non-bloodborne pathogens, those working or having facilities in California will be the exception. California OSHA ("CalOSHA") will issue a citation under this standard if a violation is identified during an inspection. CalOSHA's standard can be found at https://www.dir.ca.gov/title8/5199-1.html.

Workers' Rights

Workers are entitled a workplace free from harm. They have a right to file a complaint without fear of retaliation. Remember as you are building, revising, and expanding your occupational health programs to include these elements prominently into your written plans.

The OSHA Poster is required to be posted where employees can see it. The poster – "Job Safety and Health; It's the Law!" is available on OSHA's website (https://www.osha.gov/Publications/osha3165.pdf) and includes what all workers have the right to do including the right to a safe workplace, filing a confidential complaint, requesting copies of OSHA citations issued, and more.

It also includes requirements of what employers must do, including providing employees a workplace free from recognized hazards, providing required training, and compliance with OSHA standards, as well as additional compliance information. The poster also provides OSHA's confidential phone line: 1-800-321-OSHA.

Employee Access to Medical Records

The purpose of the OSHA standard 29 CFR 1910.1020 *Access to employee exposure and medical records* is "to provide employees and their designated representatives a right of access to relevant exposure and medical records…to yield both direct and indirect improvements in the detection, treatment, and prevention of occupational disease" (OSHA 2011a).

Medical records specific to infectious disease can include vaccination or immunization records, post-exposure medical follow-up and prophylaxis, biological monitoring, medical evaluation for respirator fit testing, and more.

Maintaining confidentiality of records can get complicated especially when an employee health department sits within the broader infrastructure of a healthcare facility. The authorized person maintaining records has an important job protecting the health information of its employees. Just as HIPAA laws are in place to protect patient confidentiality, Access to Medical Records standard is in place to protect employees. The HIPAA privacy rule does not cover workers' compensation cases, even when the worker becomes the "patient," so adherence to this OSHA standard becomes even more important.

Since the world is learning more about the impact a pandemic like COVID-19 can have on workplaces, it is important to consider that if a facility is performing employee temperature-taking or contact tracing, these records could be considered applicable under the standard. As such, determining whether or not these practices and records should be kept confidential is a critical decision-making factor. Consult with a healthcare practitioner when deciding how to handle these practices and protocols. Always side on keeping employee names and identifiers off records that are going to be shared outside of the occupational health provider themselves if it is unclear what confidentiality requirements are pertinent.

Since employee exposure and medical records need to be kept confidential from the employer, Boxes 5.4 and 5.5 provide tools, resources, prophylaxis, and record-keeping guidance, as well as what to do if there is an exposure.

Box 5.4 Tools and Resources
- CDC Exposure to Blood, What Healthcare Personnel Need to Know https://www.cdc.gov/hai/pdfs/bbp/Exp_to_Blood.pdf
- Infection Prevention & Control Orientation Self-Study Guide. Department Rancho Los Amigos National Rehabilitation Center Infection Prevention & Control 2010 Edition (Revised 2014) http://file.lacounty.gov/SDSInter/dhs/218120_SLM.InfControl.withposttestonly.RevMay2014.pd
- Joint Commission Standards (available for purchase at https://www.joint-commission.org/standards_information/standards.aspx)

Box 5.5 Post-Exposure Prophylaxis and Recordkeeping Resources
- PEP (Post-exposure Prophylaxis) Line. 888-HIV-4911. http://nccc.ucsf. edu/clinician-consultation/pep-post-exposure-prophylaxis/
- Resources for Management and Treatment Guidelines for Bloodborne Infectious Diseases: HIV/AIDS, HEPATITIS B, HEPATITIS C (NIOSH). https://www.cdc.gov/niosh/topics/bbp/guidelines.html
- Updated U.S. Public Health Service guidelines for the management of occupational exposures to HIV and recommendations for postexposure prophylaxis. https://stacks.cdc.gov/view/cdc/20711

References

CDC. (n.d.). *Exposed to HIV Infographic.* https://www.cdc.gov/hai/pdfs/HIV/ HIVPEPinfographicFINAL.pdf

EPINet International Safety Center. (2019). EPINet Report for Sharp Object Injury and Blood and Body Fluid Exposures.

NIOSH. (2020). Respirator Trusted-Source Information. https://www.cdc.gov/niosh/npptl/topics/ respirators/disp_part/RespSource.html

OSHA. (2001). Bloodborne Pathogens Standard. 29 CFR 1910.1030.

OSHA. (2011a). Access to employee exposure and medical records. 29 CFR 1910.1020.

OSHA. (2011b). Respiratory Protection Standard. 29 CFR 1910.134.

OSHA. (2013). Hazard Communication Standard. 29 CFR 1910.1200.

OSHA. (2020). Recordkeeping Rule. 29 CFR 1904.

Chapter 6
Other Regulatory Requirements, National Standards, and Accreditation

Objectives
- List Federal Agencies and Accreditation Bodies that provide requirements and recommendations for exposure to infectious disease.
- Describe essential components for compliance with standards and guidance.

Department of Transportation

It may sound surprising that the US Department of Transportation (DOT) would have regulations in place that address workplace infectious disease risks in health care. They do. If you consider that OSHA regulates what is in the workplace and DOT regulates everything that leaves the workplace and is – in transit to and used or disposed of – at another workplace. In a sense this includes everything that has the potential to pose as a hazard to those working or traveling on the roads and rails. The Federal Aviation Administration (FAA) also has purview over those who work by air.

This includes specifically provisions (49 CFR 173.197) for labeled and packaging regulated medical or biohazard items and waste; potentially infectious materials (biological samples or products); or waste generated from health care and sent to other healthcare facilities, laboratories, research institutions, landfills, or waste streams. Included here are not just sharps containers and "red bag" waste but also waste products from surgery, autopsy, or other potentially infectious materials.

Biological products that may be infectious – blood products, specimens, cultures, live vaccines, and diagnostic specimens – must be transported safely because if they are compromised, they could expose a worker coming into contact with them. Transportation of infectious substances affecting humans and animals, including regulated medical waste, including labeling and packaging for these items are regulated by the DOT Hazardous Materials Rule (HM226A, Hazardous Materials Regulations (HMR; 49 CFR parts 171–180). Mailing is regulated by the US Postal Service (68 FR 33858) and harmonized with DOT (71 FR 32244).

© Springer Nature Switzerland AG 2020
A. H. Mitchell, *Preventing Occupational Exposures to Infectious Disease in Health Care*, https://doi.org/10.1007/978-3-030-56039-3_6

If receiving or shipping any "infectious materials" via private carrier (FedEx, UPS, etc.) or the US Postal Service, be sure to identify what regulations need to be followed for packaging and labeling so that the safest controls are put into place to protect all those that may come into contact with the package and its contents. Most times this is as simple as ensuring the container is sealed and leakproof and adequately labeled as "diagnostic specimen" or a "biological sample."

US Environmental Protection Agency

Here is an interesting note on the U.S. Environmental Protection Agency (EPA). The Federal EPA does not cover regulated or biohazard waste and has not since the early 1990s (Medical Waste Tracking Act, 1988). Rather they rely on state environmental agencies and departments of health to do this.

Disposal of infectious waste can become a real public health hazard, especially when thinking about multidrug resistant organisms. If there is a potential for infectious disease waste generated from healthcare facilities to penetrate the groundwater or soil that nourishes food crops or food animals, it can negatively impact human, animal, and plant health.

The intricacies of the human microbiome will not be covered here, but in short, pathogenic microorganisms and the antimicrobials designed to treat them – if released improperly – can have an impact on our biochemistry based on what is ingested/eaten. There is a reliance on the naturally occurring "good" bacteria to keep us healthy and fight off bad bacteria. If that natural balance is disturbed by not paying attention to the way infectious and chemical waste are disposed, there is a risk of compromising health.

It is important to note that if a facility performs instrument sterilization using a method like ethylene oxide, for example, there are regulations in place to prevent emissions of toxics into the air. These emissions can potentially impact the community and environment (EPA 2007). To date, there have been class action suits filed about these very issues that have been successful.

Centers for Disease Control and Prevention

Perhaps the best-known guidance and resources on preventing infectious disease transmission are from the Centers for Disease Control and Prevention (CDC). The lion's share of the Agency's guidance is targeted at preventing patient or healthcare-associated infections (HAIs), chronic disease, and vaccine-preventable diseases in the general public, but they do have some guidance on preventing occupational illness and infection that will be summarized here.

> **Box 6.1 CDC Guidance Documents for Post-exposure Prophylaxis and Immunization**
> - Viral Hepatitis – Prevention in Health Care
> - Information for Healthcare Personnel Potentially Exposed to Hepatitis C Virus (HCV) – Recommended Testing and Follow-up
> - Post-exposure prophylaxis, Hepatitis B
> - Post-exposure prophylaxis (HIV and other bloodborne pathogens)
> - Immunization of Health-Care Personnel: Recommendations of the Advisory Committee on Immunization Practices (ACIP)

Exposure to bloodborne pathogens and OSHA compliance was covered in depth in the previous chapter. It mentioned guidance for post-exposure follow-up when an employee sustains an injury or needlestick from a contaminated sharp or a BBFE. Therefore, it seems most appropriate to start with CDC's guidance here.

CDC has several guidance documents and resources for management and treatment of occupational HIV, HBV, and HCV. Since time is of the essence after an exposure, CDC's guidance focuses on receiving prompt attention immediately following a mucocutaneous incident.

Guidance documents (listed in Box 6.1) address not just prevention tactics (most outlined above from OSHA) but also steps an employee needs to take following an exposure, as well as clinical guidance and instructions on testing, diagnostics, and treatment for occupational health and infectious disease nurses and physicians.

Since the occupational transmission of Ebola virus cases in Dallas, Texas in 2014, CDC has spent recent years focused on developing and publishing guidance for exposures to extremely infectious high-mortality pathogens like Ebola and now COVID-19. Guidance focuses on performance parameters, selection, and proper donning/doffing protocols for PPE. The public often gets frustrated with CDC since they change and update information frequently based on what they know at the time. This can confuse guidance offered from one day to the next. We saw this unfold with the COVID-19 pandemic and it will surely arise as new treatments and vaccines become available.

CDC's guidance for infectious disease ranges from triaging, managing, and evaluating suspected or known infected patients to providing direction to emergency and first responders, environmental services, outpatient and ambulatory centers, hospitals and acute care, as well as managing specimens in the laboratory.

When thinking about pathogens as virulent as Ebola, stay calm and remember that being educated and prepared is 99.9% of the work. In the event an outbreak occurs in countries like the United States, you will have ready access to the how-to's at your fingertips. This starts with strict adherence to standard precautions and ongoing practice with donning, doffing, and safely containerizing contaminated PPE and lots and lots of hand washing and drying.

Aside from Ebola and COVID-19, CDC does offer guidance on isolation precautions for infectious agents, but again its focus is almost wholly on preventing transmission from environment or staff to patients rather than vice versa. Regardless, the same concepts hold true.

Guideline for Isolation Precautions: Preventing Transmission of Infectious Agents in Healthcare Settings

The *Guideline for Isolation Precautions: Preventing Transmission of Infectious Agents in Healthcare Settings* (CDC 2007) is intended to be used by infection prevention staff, healthcare epidemiologists, and healthcare administration to develop, implement, and evaluate infection prevention and control programs across the continuum of care. Mostly isolation precautions pertain to healthcare-associated pathogens from multidrug-resistant organisms (MDROs) that result in patient HAIs. These MDROs are spread via direct contact from environmental surfaces, hands, medical devices, airborne, or droplet and include those identified in Chap. 4, such as MRSA, MSSA, Acinetobacter, *C. difficile*, and tuberculosis. This guidance does also address:

- Infectious acts of weaponized or massively distributed (public drinking water or food sources) bioterrorism, including anthrax, smallpox, and plague, to name a few
- Emerging infectious diseases like Severe Acute Respiratory Syndrome (SARS), Monkeypox, Hemorrhagic Fever Viruses (Ebola, Marburg), and Dengue and Yellow Fevers

One of the greatest elements of this document is that it has suggestions and recommendations for a variety of healthcare environments including not just hospitals but high-risk units within hospitals like burn units, ICUs, pediatrics, and community-based settings like ambulatory centers and long-term care.

Important elements in these guidance documents include precautions for clinical, laboratory, and environmental services personnel, PPE selection and use, handling and processing linen and laundry, and managing waste.

Guidelines for Infection Control in Healthcare Personnel

Finally, a collaborative team of experts from CDC, NIOSH, and its partner organizations provide recommendations specifically for healthcare personnel in its 2019 publication *Guidelines for Infection Control in Healthcare Personnel* (CDC 2019) designed to provide methods for reducing the transmission of infections from patients to healthcare personnel and from healthcare personnel to patients. This guidance is extremely detailed, and it is recommended that if you do not have responsibility for the administration of personnel immunization and clinical services, you share it with those who do. The document can be found in its entirety at https://www.cdc.gov/infectioncontrol/pdf/guidelines/infection-control-HCP-H.pdf

The 1998 guidance was published at a time when there were just shy of 9 million Americans working in health care and now that number exceeds 20 million – in fact one in nearly eight people is employed by the healthcare sector (Kaiser Family

Foundation 2015). The guidance was updated in 2019 to be more generalized, providing high-level programmatic recommendations rather than hazard-specific recommendations. However, despite the fact that guidance has been in place for decades, not much is new. This is because what was known then still rings true.

CDC's guidance includes useful tips for leadership, management, and occupational health services leaders and staff about considerations for personnel health services departments to include sufficient resources for leadership and management, communication and collaboration, assessment of risks, medical evaluations, education and training, immunization programs, management of exposures, and management of health records.

An effective department needs to conduct the following services and considerations in addition to those listed above, including:

(a) Coordination with other departments (e.g., infection prevention, risk management, supply chain, environmental health and safety, contractor services, operations, environmental services (EVS), human resources, etc.)
(b) Autonomy of decision-making and processes for non-compliance
(c) Integration between patient safety and worker safety
(d) Management of job-related illnesses and exposures to infectious diseases, including policies for work restrictions for infected or exposed personnel
(e) Counseling services for personnel on infection risks related to employment or special conditions
(f) Occupational incident surveillance and recordkeeping
(g) Process for employee feedback, evaluation, and review

The organization of the department needs to take into consideration the size of the facility, the population it serves, the services it offers, and the employee type (contract, temporary, specialty, etc.). There needs to be coordination with other departments and committees including infection prevention and control, materials management, facilities/operations, risk management/loss control, community/public relations, and others.

An essential component to occupational infectious disease prevention is maintaining vaccination programs and records. CDC offers the immunization recommendations for all healthcare personnel on their website for free: Immunization of Health-Care Personnel Recommendations of the Advisory Committee on Immunization Practices (ACIP) (https://www.cdc.gov/mmwr/pdf/rr/rr6007.pdf).

The guidance includes immunization practices for hepatitis B, influenza, measles, mumps, rubella, meningococcus, pertussis, tetanus, diphtheria, typhoid, and varicella (CDC 2011). There are recommendations for people with "special certain conditions" like pregnant women or those who have underlying disease or chronic conditions like diabetes. It is important to consider these special considerations as the goal is to make sure healthcare personnel remain healthy and well when exposed and not to impart any additional hardship, illness, or negative adverse effect.

Like all of the regulations, guidance documents, and recommended practices highlighted in this chapter, there are also suggested practices and controls for PPE use, environmental cleaning and disinfection, work restrictions should an exposure occur, and even suggested protocols if there are allergies or sensitivities to vaccines, latex, or other potential adverse events.

A trend is emerging in all of these documents and guidelines. Though each Federal Agency has guidance of its own, they all reflect tried and true standard precautions, engineering and work practice controls, PPE use, labeling, laundering, cleaning, disinfecting, sterilizing, training, and communication of hazards to personnel, patients, and the public. Whether it is your job to protect personnel, patients, or the public in your role, the concepts, actions, and protections are nearly all the same.

There are likely additional requirements in your state, county, and city; therefore, it is important to stay abreast of what is required in your area as it pertains to reportable diseases/illnesses, licensure, accreditation, annual reports, and more. At the time of writing this book, it is uncertain if a vaccine will be available for SARS-CoV-2 (COVID-19 disease). If there is one, it is likely that it will be recommended for not only people with underlying co-morbidities but also for healthcare workers.

National Institute for Occupational Safety and Health (NIOSH)

While the National Institute for Occupational Safety and Health (NIOSH) is not a regulatory agency, it is an important one relative to preventing occupational exposure to infectious disease. It is considered a "sister" agency to OSHA as both were born out of the Occupational Safety and Health Act (OSH Act) of 1970. OSHA is regulatory, NIOSH is research and advocacy based. It sits within the CDC and is a research and outreach agency with focus on providing evidence-based recommendations for protecting workers. They have terrific resources for program building and education available on their website, including information on emerging infectious diseases (https://www.cdc.gov/niosh/topics/emerginfectdiseases/) and blood-borne diseases (https://www.cdc.gov/niosh/topics/bbp/).

NIOSH also certifies all respirators. Their respiratory protection program is robust and detailed. The Hospital Respiratory Protection Program Toolkit is a useful resource for hospital administrators responsible for employee respiratory protection (NIOSH 2015).

The Joint Commission

The Joint Commission (TJC) (formerly known as the Joint Commission for Accreditation of Healthcare Organizations or "JAYCO") establishes quality standards for the accreditation of healthcare facilities. Joint Commission standards are not laws because they are not a regulatory body. Joint Commission is a volunteer compliance service that healthcare organizations pay for so that they can gain access to a host of factors or considerations like Medicare/Medicaid reimbursement differentials, marketing, quality, consistency, or status.

Just because Joint Commission standards are voluntary does not mean that they do not set very important parameters for safety and health in health care. In fact, even though it is a paid-member service, the Joint Commission often carries more weight and influence than other similar types of quality compliance. In essence, it drives national and international (Joint Commission International) standards for biological, chemical, and physical safety measures. This includes guidance for life safety, in the form of fire, flood, and natural disasters.

Joint Commission standards related to occupational infectious disease will not be showcased here because the standards are only available for purchase. They include standards for hospitals, doctor's offices, nursing homes, office-based surgery centers, behavioral health treatment facilities, and providers of home care services.

They are best known for their stellar work on performance and accountability measures, including National Patient Safety Goals that often include one or more infectious disease-specific measurement goals. One such goal is their Goal 7: Reduce the risk of healthcare-associated infections (Joint Commission 2019). Joint Commission also offers interpretations of their standard measures and goals to help their accredited facilities to achieve compliance. They have a very useful guide called "Implementing Hospital Respiratory Protection Programs: Strategies from the Field" available on their website https://www.jointcommission.org/resources/patient-safety-topics/infection-prevention-and-control/respiratory-protection/hospital-respiratory-protection-resources-and-projects/.

Overall, Joint Commission has been a beacon for promoting quality care and accountability both for safety and fiscal responsibility, and others like The Leapfrog Group and National Quality Forum have followed suit. Pay attention to these groups because they help healthcare facilities put their money where their mouth is, and hold them accountable for protecting not only the patients and communities they serve, but the healthcare personnel they employ.

Additional Regulatory and Accreditation Organizations There are additional organizations that create and publish standards specific to a healthcare delivery type – like long-term care, home care, or clinical laboratories. These include but are not limited to Accreditation Association for Ambulatory Health Care (AAAHC), Accreditation Commission for Home Care, Inc. (ACHC), and the National Accrediting Agency for Clinical Laboratory Sciences (NAACLS).

Accreditation becomes an important element in driving quality care. There are other quality-based organizations like the Leapfrog Group and National Quality Forum that are beginning to take on worker safety initiatives. This is long overdue.

Focus on patients is of paramount importance, but we know that in order to best care for our patients, we must close the gap between patient and worker safety and care for them both equally (Binder, Leapfrog Group 2017).

The US Food and Drug Administration (FDA) clears medical devices, surgical instruments, and some PPE, but their regulations are not covered here as they mostly apply to manufacturers and not to healthcare institutions themselves. The FDA website has more information on regulations for medical devices (https://www.fda.gov/medical-devices) and infectious diseases (https://www.fda.gov/about-fda/center-drug-evaluation-and-research-cder/office-infectious-diseases-oid).

References

Binder, L., & Favret, B. (2017). Closing the gap between health care worker and patient safety. *American Journal of Medical Quality, 32*(6), 679–681.

CDC. (2007). *Guideline for isolation precautions: Preventing transmission of infectious agents in healthcare settings.* https://www.cdc.gov/infectioncontrol/pdf/guidelines/isolation-guidelines-H.pdf

CDC. (2011, November 25). Morbidity and Mortality Weekly Report. *Immunization of Health-Care Personnel Recommendations of the Advisory Committee on Immunization Practices (ACIP).* https://www.cdc.gov/mmwr/pdf/rr/rr6007.pdf

CDC. (2019). *Infection control in healthcare personnel: Infrastructure and routine practices for occupational infection prevention and control services.* https://www.cdc.gov/infectioncontrol/pdf/guidelines/infection-control-HCP-H.pdf

Environmental Protection Agency. (2007). Hospital ethylene oxide sterilizers: National Emission Standards for Hazardous Air Pollutants (NESHAP).

National Institute for Occupational Safety and Health. (2015). Hospital respiratory protection program toolkit. https://www.cdc.gov/niosh/docs/2015-117/default.html.

The Joint Commission. (2019). National Patient Safety Goals 2019. Hospital Accreditation Program. https://www.jointcommission.org/assets/1/6/NPSG_Chapter_HAP_Jan2019.pdf

Chapter 7
Performing a Hazard Assessment and Building an Exposure Control Plan

Objectives
- Identify critical elements needed to perform a hazard assessment.
- List considerations to include in a job hazard analysis.
- Outline requirements of an Exposure Control Plan.
- Provide guidance on performing task assessments and audits.

Whether you are revamping your infectious disease safety and health plan, taking on new job responsibilities, or building one from scratch, there are fundamental steps, actions, and plans that need to be taken. This chapter provides the basis for the crafting, updating, expanding, or re-writing of those analyses and plans and will offers some unique ideas for creating higher standards in safety and health.

Ultimately, there are five critical elements that need to be in place for the development, execution, and compliance to have a successful occupational infectious disease safety and health program:

- Management leadership (top-down and bottom-up)
- Employee involvement
- Worksite and job task analyses
- Hazard prevention and control
- Safety and health education and training

This *Practical Guide* covers many of the elements needed to be successful in each of these areas. The best laid plans are ones that have not only high-quality ownership and accountability but also ones that are clearly written, laid out, documented, and referenced. They are ones that provide "A HA" moments for colleagues that you present them to. These plans, assessment, and analyses become the ground

© Springer Nature Switzerland AG 2020
A. H. Mitchell, *Preventing Occupational Exposures to Infectious Disease in Health Care*, https://doi.org/10.1007/978-3-030-56039-3_7

work for identifying hazards and determining the type and extent of resources needed to protect personnel, patients, and ultimately the leaderships' bottom line.

Striving for consistency, thoroughness, and method protects not only you or your department but also your management and their stakeholders. Take the time to do this part right and a great deal of focus and thought. It will serve you well.

Think of hazard assessments as volumes of an encyclopedia. Each book has different content, but the research, methodology, information, and format are consistent from one to the next. It would not be prudent to have an extremely well-documented assessment plan for exit plans in case of fire and piecemeal and an off-the-cuff plan for infectious disease. The Fire Marshall would not be available to help draw up infectious disease plans like she would for fire, which is why it is even more important to utilize the resources like this one that are available.

Hazard assessments and analyses are done to identify and document actual and potential hazards in a workplace (what is and what may be). They are intended not only to capture what, where, and when they are but also what measures are taken to prevent them. For many documented hazards and their subsequent OSHA standards, this is typically done to determine which or what PPE is best suited for each hazard and the circumstances surrounding that potential hazard and how the employer has made that determination.

For the person responsible for documenting the execution of a hazard assessment essentially, the following are required to be on the documentation:

• Occupation of person performing assessment
• Date(s) of the hazard assessment
• Name of the person performing the hazard assessment

Having the right person with the right experience and credentials performing the hazard assessment is important because the employer is responsible for compliance with local, state, and federal laws and employees rely on their employer to provide the safest possible working environment. This person can be the key to identifying what exposures may exist and how to control for them.

Since hazard assessments are required by OSHA, it is important that they are done initially (when a potential hazard is introduced) and then updated annually if there are any changes, updates, edits, or deletions needed.

Job Hazard Analysis

Hazard assessments are focused on the hazards themselves. In the case of this *Practical Guide*, bloodborne pathogens, microorganisms that cause infection and illness, infectious and communicable diseases are the hazards being addressed. In addition to a general hazard assessment, Job Hazard Analyses should be performed. These focus on the job, task, or worker rather on the hazard itself. For example, these include the hazards associated with being a physician, nurse, laboratorian, environmental services worker, sterile processor, security guard, and more.

This is different still for personnel performing jobs or tasks in different departments. The hazards associated with technicians' or technologists' jobs or tasks in a radiation/oncology unit are different than an infectious disease unit is different than in a phlebotomy unit is different than those in a clinical or research lab.

OSHA has useful resources and publications for performing and documenting job hazard analyses, and they astutely compare performing these analyses to detective work.

It is suggested that during the analyses, identify the following for each job and/or task:

- What can go wrong?
- What are the consequences?
- How could the consequence arise?
- What are the direct contributing factors to those consequences?
- What are the indirect or other possible contributing factors?
- How likely is it that the hazard will occur during the course of that job?
- How likely is it that the hazard will occur given those contributing factors and/or despite controls being in place?

A good job hazard analysis incorporates the exercise of going through likely and even unlikely possible scenarios to identify what is going on in that job or department, what precipitates the hazard, what can happen because of that hazard, etc. Some call this worst-case scenario planning, and in the case of infectious disease, this is important.

What if a patient arrives in the emergency department with a known infectious disease and the correct PPE is not available? What if it is available but during the course of treatment it fails? What if there is a terribly upset family member with that patient and they cause a scenario where violence may occur, potentially exposing several staff members and/or visitors?

Many of these scenarios unfolded in healthcare institutions around the world during the COVID-19 pandemic in a very public way. They resulted in devastating exposures and illnesses and sometimes death.

We may all be prepared in perfectly normal conditions. Something, however, many consider during public health preparedness planning, such as for future outbreaks and pandemics – wouldn't worst-case scenario job hazard analysis prove beneficial given all else that may be unknown or unanticipated at the time?

Hazard Assessment Matrix

An additional tool and another useful approach to use in addition to a hazard assessment and job hazard analysis is a hazard matrix. This comes in handy for identifying priority and focus areas. We all want to do everything, but sometimes it's important to focus where the biggest impact can be made and move on to controlling more improbable events later.

Table 7.1 Job hazard analysis matrix

Frequency of occurrence resulting in risk	Risk hazard category		
	Critical	Serious	Minor
Frequent/often	Unacceptable	Unacceptable	High
Occasional	Unacceptable	High	High
Sporadic/sometimes	Unacceptable	High	Moderate
Probable/infrequent	Moderate	Moderate	Low
Remote/improbable	Moderate	Low	Low

The matrix is designed to illustrate categories of risk (Table 7.1). It is built to identify/document the hazard, the frequency of occurrences or potential exposures to that hazard, and the severity of the outcome given the frequency of the event.

For example, if the hazard is multidrug-resistant tuberculosis, the jobs, professions, locations of care, and assigned tasks are going to vary. The hazard is the same, but the frequency and severity of that hazard change based on whether the location is a long-term care facility with immunocompromised residents or whether the location is in an inner city with a high prevalence of HIV or if the staff member is at the bedside or in the insurance claims department.

Here, matrices serve an institution well because they can be quickly pulled out during outbreaks, emergency situations, or even during job task or staffing changes. A potential decision-making matrix determining what to address and how urgently may look something like Table 7.1. As a nation, during the SARS-CoV-2/COVID-19 pandemic, healthcare providers were reminded that this is critically important for engineering control availability and PPE provisions.

Unacceptable risks must be addressed immediately and controls put into place as well as considerations for "crisis capacity" strategies for preparedness of an outbreak, epidemic, or pandemic. These risks may include those employees working in laboratory research for highly contagious microorganisms or frontline healthcare workers caring for patients in isolation rooms in the ICU.

High-risk categories warrant careful attention as these hazards are ongoing and high risk for exposure to infectious disease. These could include environmental services workers going in to process patient rooms that are occupied and on isolation precautions or providers performing triaging in emergency departments for patients that are symptomatic.

Moderate- and low-risk categories can be subjective depending on the specific facility. During an outbreak locally or a pandemic globally, a low-risk category like food service in a long-term care facility may become moderate or even high when there is potential exposure to people who may be symptomatic and likely to shed virus in public/common spaces.

In times of outbreak, epidemic, or pandemic it is also important to limit exposures in certain job categories that would otherwise be low risk. For example, cross-training ICU clinical personnel to also process (clean, disinfect) isolation rooms or having food service personnel leave meals outside of patient rooms to have authorized healthcare providers only enter patient room.

These are some examples, but this is in no way an exhaustive list, nor may it pertain to all healthcare workplaces or the services they provide.

Another way of assessing and documenting exposure risk is by estimating "likelihoods," for instance:

For every identified hazard affecting a specific portion of the body, indicate the likelihood of an exposure and rate it on a scale of 0 to 5 (0 = no/low risk and 5 = probable ongoing risk):

0: Exposure is infeasible
1: Exposure is improbable/unexpected
2: Exposure possible, but unlikely
3: Exposure probable/expected
4: Multiple exposures probable/expected
5: Continuous exposure probable/expected

Likelihood scales like this one, or many others available for free online, can assist not only with a general hazard or exposure assessment but also with appropriate and effective selection of PPE as further described in Chap. 10.

Similar scales can also be created for severity of risk and potential impact, including in the case of exposures in health care whether an exposure will result in no effect (0) sliding all the way up the scale to (5) likely death. A "0" might translate to touching a patient's wound with double gloves on in a peri-operative environment and a "5" might translate to prolonged direct mucocutaneous exposure to Ebola virus. This will vary greatly based on the type of exposures in one facility to the next. It will also vary based on facility type: acute care, long-term care, research laboratory, morgue, etc.

Exposure Control Plan

As it relates specifically to infectious diseases caused by bloodborne pathogens, OSHA has detailed requirements for documenting occupational exposures in a written Exposure Control Plan (ECP) (OSHA 2001a). In Chap. 5, all of the required sections of the OSHA Bloodborne Pathogens Standard are covered, so here we will cover what is explicitly required for the ECP. There is also a model Exposure Control Plan to use and adapt in Appendix B.

Every employer in every workplace is required by regulation to make and maintain a written ECP that includes the schedule and method of implementation for all the paragraphs of the Standard.

Paragraph

(d) Methods of Compliance

   • Engineering controls
   • Work practice controls

- Handwashing facilities, handwashing practices
- Sharps safety, sharps disposal
- Regulated waste disposal, handling
- PPE use, accessibility, disposal, laundering, repair, replacement
- Environmental services (k.n.a. housekeeping)
- Laundry

(e) HIV and HBV Research Laboratories and Production Facilities
(f) Hepatitis B Vaccination and Post-Exposure Evaluation and Follow-Up
(g) Communication of Hazards to Employees

- Training and education; new employees and annual
- Signage
- Labeling

(h) Recordkeeping

Within each of those paragraphs, there are additional requirements from the standard including:

- Procedures in place for evaluating exposure incidents
- Ensuring a copy is accessible to employees on all shifts and in all locations
- Plan is reviewed and updated at least annually and whenever there are changes (e.g., new/revised employee positions, new potential exposures, new equipment, etc.)
- Plan must reflect changes in technology that eliminate/reduce exposure (e.g., implementation of new safety-engineered devices)
- Documentation of annual consideration of those new commercially available technologies
- Documentation of the solicitation of input from non-managerial employees who are at risk of exposures

If a facility is inspected, this is one of the first documents a Compliance Safety and Health Officer (CSHO) will ask for, so it is critically important that this is maintained, readily accessible, and accurate. It is your recipe book, your Bible, your map, your guide. And it is not only yours but your employees – each and every one of them with actual or potential exposure to blood and body fluids.

The ECP will be based on what OSHA calls an "exposure determination" similar to the assessments and analyses mentioned already, but this is specific to exposure to bloodborne pathogens that may be present in blood, body fluids, and other potentially infectious materials (Table 7.2). The elements that are required to be documented are:

- A list of all job classifications in which *all* employees in those job classifications have occupational exposure;
- A list of job classifications in which *some* employees have occupational exposure
- A list of all tasks and procedures or groups of closely related task and procedures in which occupational exposure occurs and that is performed by employees (including those "all" and "some")

Table 7.2 Mucocutaneous blood and body fluid (infectious disease) exposure incident log

Date	Type of Exposure (Nose, Eyes, Mouth, Non-Intact Skin, Other)	Work Area, Department, or Unit Where Exposure Occurred	Brief Description of Exposure Incident	Type of PPE Worn During Exposure (Eye Protection, Mask, Respirator, Gown, etc.)	Would Institution of an Additional Control have Prevented the Exposure? (Y/N)

This exposure determination has to be made without regard to the use or protection of PPE. Remember, PPE is the least effective method of control, and your determination must be made on risk without PPE. These requirements come directly from 29 CFR 1910.1030 – the standard itself.

In its Compliance Directive, OSHA offers a Model Exposure Control Plan that is available online at https://www.osha.gov/OshDoc/Directive_pdf/CPL_2-2_69_ APPD.pdf (OSHA 2001b). If you are starting out, this is great news because OSHA has done much of the work for you.

As part of that Plan, they have also included a Model Sharps Injury Log. This Log is required by the Standard and must be used every time there is an occupational exposure incident involving a contaminated sharp or needlestick. You will find this Log as well as sample OSHA 300, 300A, and 301 logs in the Appendices.

OSHA does not require that employers keep a log for mucocutaneous exposures (eyes, nose, mouth, and non-intact skin), other than what is required to be kept on the OSHA 300, 300A, and 301 logs, but it may be a good idea to use one that is available like EPINet (https://internationalsafetycenter.org/use-epinet/) or to create your own that looks similar to the Sharps Injury Log. Keeping records specific to these types of exposures means that you have all the information required to know where exposures are occurring, how they are occurring, and if adequate PPE plans are in place. Regular review of a log like this allows you to fine-tune programs on a monthly, quarterly, or annual basis.

There are other useful model plans available on the World Wide Web. NIOSH has resources on its "Bloodborne Infectious Diseases" webpage. CDC also has model plans. WHO created several decision trees for humanitarian emergencies like floods and earthquakes. They serve as great model plans for regular and ongoing occupational infectious disease and risk characterization. Table 7.3 can serve as a model risk assessment plan that can be adapted for any type of event that can cause occupational exposures to infectious disease and/or caring for patients with infectious disease, including natural disasters, outbreak, pandemics, acts of terrorism, and seasonal events like flu.

Additional information can be added to incorporate information about what PPE has been selected based on risk, what work practice controls are established, and who owns responsibility for the governing policies (administrative controls) in place.

Table 7.3 Risk assessment for infectious diseases

Step	Main qualitative assessment(s)
1. Defining the event	Natural disaster Outbreak Epidemic Pandemic Terrorism Spill, off-gas (e.g., laboratory-based) Seasonal (e.g., flu)

2. Threat
Likelihood of impact/illness/infection
	Employee
	    Job/task
	    Frequency of exposure (work, home)
	    Vaccine, immunization status
	    Work practices
	    Personal practices
	    Availability of PPE
	    Ongoing access to education, training
	    Underlying health effects, comorbidities
	Agent/microorganism
	    Contact, environmental heartiness/persistence
	    Aerosol, airborne
	    Seasonal? Epidemic, pandemic
	    Resistance to treatment, disinfectant
	    Work-related, community-associated
	    Location-specific (heat, humidity, water, etc.)

3. Environmental/institutional Facility-based risk	Hierarchy of controls Institutional culture of safety Administrative controls, staffing Air exchanges, ventilation Availability of engineering controls Availability of PPE Access to PPE Education, training Waste disposal Robustness of occupational/employee health programs Incident/exposure surveillance Purchasing, supply chain

4. Assigning risk, mobilizing action	Using considerations of above to assess risk
	    Critical/catastrophic
	    High
	    Moderate
	    Low
	    None
	    Unknown

Task Assessments and Audits

Designing and performing hazard and exposure assessments are the initial and intermediate steps; in addition ongoing evaluations, audits, and "inspections" will keep programs sustainable, relevant, and effective. It is important to determine reasonable timeframes to do "rounds," once per month, once per quarter. Choose a time increment that is realistic, as well as to those that may need to be interviewed and consulted.

In performing rounds or "rounding," creating a checklist like Table 7.4 may be helpful. Included is a sample of what detail may be involved when doing audits and interviews.

Performing a job hazard analysis is an essential tool that can be done after hazards and availability and use of preventive controls are in place. For a new or first assessment, a chart-like Box 7.1 can be used. It also can be useful for ongoing or annual assessments if processes, job duties, or hazards change or are mitigated.

Table 7.4 Occupational infection prevention and control rounding checklist

Strong (S) Moderate (M) Weak (W)	Department/ Unit	Responsible Person	Engineering Control (e.g. Safer Medical Device) Use	PPE Placement/ Use	Infectious/ Medical / Sharps Waste Program	Training & Education	Changes Needing Revision? (e.g. new procedure, phased out process)	Notes
S	Operating Room (OR)	A Mitchell	Safety scalpels in place since 2014, introducing new skin closure technologies. Revisit in 2 months.	All in place and disposal adequate. No changes needed.	All in place. Sharps injury from suture left on floor, work with OR manager to identify better disposal practice.	Annual training in place. When new skin closure devices are incorporated, recheck on effectiveness of training program.	New skin closure safer devices. Ensure process is in place for employee feedback/evaluation of device.	Dr. Safety is retiring in 2018, make sure continuity plan is in place prior to her departure.

Box 7.1 Sample Simple Job Hazard Analysis Form

Job location: Emergency department	Analyst: Jane Safety	Date:

1. Task Description: Clinician performs blood collection procedure.
2. Hazard Description: Drawing capillary, venous, or arterial blood samples using a needle. Using a blood collection device (straight needle on vacuum tube or butterfly/winged steel needle or lancet), while drawing blood can result in a contaminated needlestick and exposure to a bloodborne or infectious pathogen.
3. Hazard Controls:

   1. Alert others nearby that a procedure is being performed.
   2. Alert the patient that they will feel a stick and must stay still.
   3. Don gloves.
   4. Evaluate and use a blood collection device with a injury prevention-engineered feature attached.
   5. Activate the safety feature upon completion of the procedure.
   6. Immediately dispose of the used device in a sharps container.

Tools and Resources

CDC. *Correctional Health Care Facilities Exposure Control Plan.* https://www.cdc.gov/niosh/topics/correctionalhcw/plan.html

Contra Costa County. *Communicable Diseases Exposure Control Plan.* 2012. https://cchealth.org/ems/pdf/communicable-disease-control-plan.pdf

Contagion Live. *The Contagion Outbreak Monitor.* http://www.contagion-live.com/outbreak-monitor

OSHA. *Bloodborne Pathogens Standard.* https://www.osha.gov/pls/oshaweb/owadisp.show_document?p_table=standards&p_id=10051

OSHA. *Bloodborne Pathogens Compliance Directive.* https://www.osha.gov/pls/oshaweb/owadisp.show_document?p_table=directives&p_id=2570

OSHA. *Job Hazard Analysis.* https://www.osha.gov/Publications/osha3071.html

OSHA. *Bloodborne Pathogens Standard Compliance Directive. Model Exposure Control Plan.* https://www.osha.gov/OshDoc/Directive_pdf/CPL_2-2_69_APPD.pdf

WHO. *Communicable Disease Risk Assessment Protocol for Humanitarian Emergencies.* 2007. http://www.who.int/diseasecontrol_emergencies/guidelines/Com_dis_risk_ass_oct07.pdf

These are intended to be very detailed, based on employee positions, responsibilities, and degree of exposure/risk.

This chapter has a variety of tools, forms, scales, and resources that can be used and tailored to any healthcare setting. They are only suggestions based on what has been used in occupational health in various healthcare settings over the years. Feel free to design one that is unique to the setting within which the assessments are being performed. Laboratory environments, research labs, pharmaceutical companies, and animal care/veterinary facilities have unique exposures and job tasks that are different than those of traditional patient care-based health care, but preventing occupational exposures to infectious disease is no less important. Use these models or build your own.

References

OSHA. (2001a). *Bloodborne pathogens standard.* https://www.osha.gov/pls/oshaweb/owadisp.show_document?p_table=standards&p_id=10051

OSHA. (2001b). *Bloodborne pathogens compliance directive.* https://www.osha.gov/pls/oshaweb/owadisp.show_document?p_table=directives&p_id=2570

World Health Organization. (2007). *Three step communicable disease risk assessment.* http://www.who.int/diseasecontrol_emergencies/guidelines/Com_dis_risk_ass_oct07.pdf

World Health Organization. (2008). Managing Humanitarian Response in the Field.

Chapter 8
Institutional and Administrative Controls

Objectives
- Describe how individualized health beliefs can drive safer occupational outcomes.
- Discuss the differences between safety culture and safety climate.
- Identify cues to action for safe work practices.
- Describe opportunities to "teach up" to leadership.
- Establish strategies for communicating cost and value of programs.

In safety and health professions, safety controls are traditionally addressed as what risk can be physically "engineered" out. In other words, how do we physically make a workplace safer with ventilation; railings on raised platforms, risers, or stairs; glass/plexiglass dividers for security in emergency departments; metal detectors; physical containment for construction remediation; and more. Prevention is phrased in the form of a hierarchy of controls that include physical elimination, substitution, engineering controls, PPE, and actions that individuals can take – work practice controls.

Most proactive, safe working environments focus not only top-down too but more "abstract" to functional. It is often the *culture* or *climate* of the institution and its administration that set the stage for what controls exist at all levels. Institutions must understand what drives individual behavior (outside of physical controls) – including personal, professional, and financial motivators – within their facility in order to provide the most health-forward infrastructure for its employees.

There is a behavior model that was developed in the 1950s designed to identify why people were not exhibiting healthy behaviors like practicing safe sex or quitting smoking. The Health Belief Model is used frequently in health care but mostly to drive health-seeking behaviors by patients, including, for example, medication adherence, home wound care, blood glucose testing, and healthful eating.

© Springer Nature Switzerland AG 2020
A. H. Mitchell, *Preventing Occupational Exposures to Infectious Disease in Health Care*, https://doi.org/10.1007/978-3-030-56039-3_8

To improve behaviors, the Health Belief Model – or HBM – addresses the link between a person's belief and their behavior. For example, if one perceives no threat from acquiring HIV from risky sexual behavior because they have been having sex for years without protection and do not currently have HIV and perhaps they do not know anyone with HIV either. Or if a healthy adult does not perceive any risk associated with becoming sick with COVID-19, they may not physically distance themselves from others. All the while thinking they would remain healthy if potentially exposed, but not considering how they may become an unintended "vector" to someone less healthy that may not be able to fight off the viral attack.

These perceptions drive a person's belief in their ability to dictate their own health-based choices. In an occupational setting, especially as it relates to infectious disease, this model has direct implications in the way we approach designing programs, plans, and campaigns.

An employee's health-related behavior depends on their perceptions in four critical areas:

1. The severity of a potential exposure resulting in an illness or infection
2. The susceptibility to that illness or infection
3. The benefits of taking a preventive action or utilizing a control
4. The barriers to taking that action or utilizing that control

Let's say that a facility is having difficulty with employees adhering to glove use and hand hygiene protocols in patient rooms on the nursing units. Identifying the root cause to this problem needs to be taken not just at the individual level but at an institutional level.

Here are some questions to ask that can help in collecting enough information to get started. Depending on the answers to these questions and if there *even* are answers, they can serve as the basis for program building, expansion, and/or revamping.

- What is the climate of safety in a facility? How do individuals perceive their safety and security when they are at work?
- What is the culture of safety? How does the organization communicate its dedication and prioritization of safety within its walls and as a member of the community?
- Does management have a flippant attitude about perceived risk of not donning and doffing gloves appropriately?
- Are they less focused on glove use and more as a preventive control and more focused on diagnostic tests and medication delivery as a "cure"?
- Do they perceive a lack of negative outcomes associated with failure to don gloves at the right time?
- What is the overall facility-wide perception about the susceptibility of transmission, illness, or infection associated with poor hand hygiene?
- Do they think that since it may only be an issue for severely immunocompromised patients and not for employees at all, does this drive individual behavior?

- Is there a perception that despite best individual efforts that the institution as a whole does not believe that hand hygiene plays into occupational risk?
- What about accessibility?

  - If an employee overcomes all of the facility's perceptions and perceives a benefit to his or her actions and choses a safe behavior anyway, are there the means to comply on their own? Or are there too many barriers?
  - Are gloves available everywhere they are needed?
  - Are sinks accessible?

- Does training illustrate the importance of timing of glove use?
- Is there peer-pressure to hurry and therefore not carry through with proper technique?
- Do colleagues with more experience serve as role models for bad habits?
- Are cues in place to drive the positive behavior?

In a study performed at Harvard University, researchers informed hotel housekeepers in a study group in seven different hotels that the daily work they do (cleaning and preparing rooms for guests) is "good exercise and satisfies the Surgeon General's recommendation for an active lifestyle" (Crum and Langer 2007). The control group was not given this information. Although none of their daily activities changed during the study period, after 4 weeks the study group of housekeepers showed a decrease in weight, blood pressure, body fat, waist-to-hip ratio, and body mass index. Researchers concluded rightly that "mindset matters" and used the premise of the HBM to prove it.

In fact, mindset and the mind's ability to drive behavior and physiology are "so powerful that it can actually change health based on a changed perspective" (Lakhiani 2016). Beliefs and symbols elicit powerful performance and outcomes, both negative and positive. Using positive cues to action as it relates to worker safety and health and the behaviors associated with safer actions, like PPE use, can work greatly in your and your facility's favor.

Operational Safety Culture

Essentially, determining the key elements to what drives safe and healthy behavior is the foundation to assessing how an institution's culture impacts overall safety within all of its operations and functions. An operational safety *culture* is made up of the attitudes, rules, conduct, superstitions, and, yes, beliefs of an organization. It encompasses how safety is thought of in the institution. It can be "safety first" or "zero tolerance" or "three strikes."

Here we discriminate between the difference of "safety culture" and its more proactive cousin, "operational safety culture." Safety culture can be containerized; department, unit, or floor dependent; even process or procedure dependent. It can have the pervasiveness throughout an institution and its operations that it needs to have to impact safety and health deeply, at its root, long-term. Operational safety culture implies an inherent, ongoing, and long lasting, all hands on deck no matter the day, time, or shift culture. A facility cannot operate (literally or figuratively) without one.

Originally, the culture of safety began in "high reliability" industries like airlines, where an obsession with potential failure is necessary because failure can mean a situation where there are mass casualties – hundreds of lives lost in one blink. There is also a reluctance to over-simplify tasks for fear that eliminating steps can result in loss of life. Many arguments have been made over the past decade that workplaces, including health care, need to adopt this rubric.

High reliability healthcare organizations create achievable paradigms in which safety is so ingrained in a culture that it becomes more like the aviation industry where no (zero) errors are acceptable. A high reliability organization does not accept the occurrence of any catastrophe, whether it be injury, illness, error, or "accident."

We agree that health care – especially as it relates to exposure to infectious disease – is a high reliability case. One failure or simplification can result in multiple exposures to infectious pathogens that can wind up as public health crises. This was true with SARS, Ebola, and may be the case with the next globally emerging pathogen.

Safety Climate

Safety *climate* is different in that it represents the feeling or mood at the time. It represents shared perceptions of workers regarding the level of safety where they work and includes how they feel about management commitment, intolerances for non-compliance, cleanliness, and accessibility of PPE. Climates while rather steady can be temporary and dynamic but when extended or prolonged can alter the overall culture too.

Safety climates can influence compliance with use of PPE and adhering to universal or standard precautions. As it relates to controls for preventing occupational exposure to infectious disease, this is exactly what we want. Positive influencers for adherence include management commitment and regular individual feedback and training (Grosch et al. 1999).

Interestingly if an employee – say a nurse – has had an exposure or illness associated with an infectious microorganism and deems that exposure/illness a hindrance to their work/job (they are on alternate duty or home for post-exposure treatment), it influences their perception of climate, whereas a nurse that has never had a recognized exposure/illness does not. This follows the logic of the HBM and has been noted in the peer-reviewed literature.

The seemingly temporary nature of safety climate can work in a positive or negative way.

If the underlying culture of safety is apathetic, a positive climate may emerge when there is a looming threat, like Ebola or COVID-19, for instance, that brings people together to prepare themselves, their patients, and their communities for positive action. In 2014, even the laxest safety cultures peaked towards a more positive safety climate at that time. Whether or not it lasted long enough to become a "habit" (18–250 days) and influence the overarching culture of safety is unique to each facility (Lally et al. 2010). EPINet data shows very poor adherence to PPE use when workers experience a blood or body fluid splash or splatter across consecutive years 2013, 2014, 2015, and 2016. This indicates that unfortunately PPE use is not a habit (ISC 2018).

On the contrary, if there is an overall positive culture of safety in an institution and there been a wave of budget cuts and layoffs, attention to safety may dip the climate at the time as employee's stress about issues other than physical protection and more about financial protection or job-stability. If there is a mad dash to prepare for a mock (or real) Joint Commission survey (or surveyor) and pull together the *perfect* plan out of thin air, your volatile climate may not be enough to hold together the matrix of your culture.

Simply – in an ideal situation – safety climates are not this fickle, and an institution's safety climate is a reflection of its culture and remains strong and stable over time. In fact, a strong culture and climate of safety positively influence how employees live their lives in and outside of work. It can have a great deal of influence on the overall community health. In the Tools and Resources section of this chapter, there are some campaigns that can be used that trickle down from workplace to community.

It is not just important that you build your facility's occupational health and safety program but also that it is built to last.

Cues to Action

In the HBM and as it relates to building (and maintaining) both a culture and climate of safety, it is critical to have the right cues of action in place for those that have safe perceptions in place and need motivators in place and for those that are not yet there but need additional cues to action. The HBM offers the ability to understand different behaviors or attitudes people may develop under the same condition by following or not following certain guidelines or requirements (Efstathiou et al. 2011).

Cues to action (Box 8.1) for these behaviors can range from simplistic to complex and can benefit those in all ranges of perceived risk/reward.

> **Cues to Action**
> - Visible, well-positioned posters
> - Ongoing individual feedback, from managers, peers, patients
> - Accessibility of PPE
> - Confidence in safer medical device, PPE use, standard precautions, etc.
> - Incentives, including financial, physical, emotional, peer-to-peer

Box 8.1

It may not be plausible to have the authority or ability to influence financial or professional advancement incentives. However, exercising autonomy as a safety and health, infection prevention, or risk management professional provides and communicates a great many cues to action. This could include creating posters and posted reminders about the importance of PPE use for employees, as well as providing ongoing feedback to leadership and administration about the importance of the location and accessibility of PPE to drive use/wear.

Leadership and staff alike may both need a small push and some encouragement from occupational infection preventionists to ensure them that small, positive changes can make big, meaningful differences relative to safety. The more cues that exist in the environment, the more likely the sustainability of a can-do culture.

Teaching Up

In occupational safety and health circles, long-time professionals, advocates, and experts typically agree that the bedrock of safer working environments ultimately boils down to two things – employer responsibility and worker empowerment. This may be an oversimplified concept since so much of infection prevention and control is focused around multifaceted, bundled approaches to protect patients – hand hygiene, surface cleaning and disinfection, decreasing indwell time of catheters, antimicrobial stewardship, diagnostic surveillance, etc. These elements work together to ensure redundancies for the safest possible outcomes as it relates to healthcare-associated infections.

For occupational health and safety, however, many argue that employers are solely responsible for providing a safe environment for their employees from floor to ceiling, wall to wall, and parking lot to patient room. They also defend the position that workers must feel empowered to speak up and speak out when their safety and health "rights" are being threatened. This would then drive employer responsibility. It's cyclical – a responsibility-empowerment windmill.

This scenario may be more true in manufacturing settings where physical hazards are more clear and the "product" of interest is a widget. It may not translate so directly in health care where the "product" is a person – a patient. As discussed in prior chapters, there is a reliance on the hierarchy of controls where hazards can be eliminated, substituted, or engineered out, but in the realm of micro- or nano-hazards, this gets more difficult. For hazards unseen by the naked eye, there is a reliance rather on the use of PPE and execution of standard, isolation, and droplet precaution practices. Here, we depend on human behavior and work practices.

This dependence on what we choose to do as individuals to protect ourselves means that we need to educate our leaders about what we need to be successful and what their responsibility is to protect their workforce. We must not lose sight of the importance of teaching up.

Just like cues of action are needed for each and every one of us to select a positive health behavior, cues are needed to be launched upward to administration and leadership. This is not just so at a facility level but also a community, state, and national level.

Collecting data about exposures and injuries becomes most important here. Surveillance drives resources and focus.

Every book, article, and publication on infection prevention and occupational health and safety state that "buy-in from leadership" is critical to overall wellness. Yes, no doubt. However, as individual's we do not feel empowered to march straight to our leaders and say... you must buy-in. In lieu of that approach, here are some immediately actionable Teaching Up Opportunities that can collectively result in the greater likelihood that leadership will buy in.

Adequate Staffing

Every productive industry and individual business relies on adequate staffing to keep its doors open. This has never been more true than in health care where adequate staffing can mean the difference between life and death for its "customers" – patients. Since most occupational health and safety and infection prevention professionals are not in the position to autonomously hire as many personnel as they think they need, this will not be addressed in much detail. Regardless, it would be remiss not to include it here as a crucial administrative control.

Adequate staffing ensures that not only patient care is the highest quality but also that employees feel empowered enough to ask for help when they need it without fear of pulling them away from another important duty. Instituting team accountability approaches can also result in co-workers and colleagues reminding each other how important it is to take care of themselves and each other. This can improve use of PPE, activation of safety mechanisms on medical devices, immediate disposal of contaminated sharps, more frequent handwashing, and more.

If staffing is not adequate, rushing, exhaustion, and a general sense of overwhelming distress cause injury, exposure, and error to both self and patient. While you may not be responsible for scheduling and hiring, it is important to understand the role that it plays in creating programs that matter, last, and work.

Establishing and Communicating Value for Occupational Infection Prevention and Control Programs

So many papers, websites, presentations, and printed materials use the fear of financial outlay for OSHA fines as a justification for driving safety programs in all sorts of industries. In health care, in addition to OSHA fines, many make the argument that non-compliance with Joint Commission surveys can severely and negatively impact not just the facility's ability to market itself but to get top reimbursement for Medicare and Medicaid patients (the driver of Joint Commission compliance).

There are also potential negative consequences from receiving poor scores or grades from quality organizations like The Leapfrog Group. This may all be true for patient safety, but because Joint Commission and other standards setting and accreditation bodies focus almost solely on patient measures, this will not drive consistent funding for occupational health programs except in the most forward thinking "early adopter" facilities which are few and far between.

Let's explore OSHA fines for a minute. The fine or penalty for a "serious" violation (e.g., failure to comply with the requirement to use engineering controls like safer medical devices) is $13,494 maximum. This can be downwardly adjusted (lessened) for those employers with no history of fines, good will to abate hazards quickly, establishment size, and more. Essentially, OSHA will give employers the benefit of the doubt when the benefit is warranted (OSHA 2020).

Fines can get as high as $34,937 (updated January 2020) for willful or repeated violations, and while this represents possibilities more so for manufacturing facilities where an injury may result in imminent death (trench collapse, fall from a building, etc.), versus health care, it may drive action.

As it relates to building occupational programs in health care though, the stick rarely works long term.

In order to get ahead of the multitude of injuries and illnesses that can occur in health care compared to other industries, OSHA has issued several National and Regional "Emphasis Programs" in hospitals and nursing and long-term care facilities available on their website (www.osha.gov) that focus on highest prevalence injuries and illnesses including:

- Musculoskeletal disorders (MSDs) relating to patient or resident handling
- Workplace violence (WPV)
- Bloodborne pathogens (BBP)
- Tuberculosis (TB)
- Slips, trips, and falls (STFs)

As you will note, two out of the top 5 occupational incidents involve infectious disease. If the fear of an OSHA inspection and subsequent fines does not drive ongoing focus on occupational health programs in your facility, sometimes educating leadership about the areas where OSHA will continue to focus in the coming decades just might. OSHA bases its emphasis on real, high hazards across all industries, and for them, health care is often first on the list.

As mentioned in the earlier chapters, healthcare employment surpasses all others in growth, and with aging populations living longer, in conjunction with growing population bases, this trend is not likely to change at all.

In fact, even today health care far surpasses any other industry when looking at nonfatal injuries and illnesses. According to the Bureau of Labor Statistics (BLS) data, the distribution of nonfatal occupational injuries and illnesses by private industry sector indicates that the health care and social assistance sector had approximately 32,700 illnesses and 544,800 injuries reported in 2018. The next highest was 35,000 illnesses and 395,300 (approximate estimation, rounded by BLS) in manufacturing and 8800 illnesses and 401,100 injuries in retail trades (BLS 2019).

The top 10 industries with the highest frequency of illnesses and injuries reported to BLS include the following (BLS 2019):

1. Health care and social assistance
2. Manufacturing
3. Retail trade
4. Accommodation and food services
5. Transportation and warehousing
6. Construction
7. Wholesale trade
8. Administrative and waste services
9. Other services (except public administration)
10. Professional and technical services

The point of all of this is to help craft messaging and the justification of ongoing support needed to sustain occupational health programs in health care, especially as it relates to high hazard exposures like those from infectious disease. We all have to fight for funding in a world with so many competing priorities and so many critical paths that must not be ignored. It is best to get past feeling awkward about having to justify it and just dive right in. It will require doing one or more of these exercises.

Low to Minimum Effectiveness Analysis

Are you in compliance with standards and satisfied that's all is needed? Do some controls and training need to get upgraded to achieve 100% compliance? Remember federal and state regulations and accreditation standards are not in place to make you a rock star; they are in place for minimum effectiveness.

They are the bear minimum an employer commits to make sure employees are safe. If your facility is in this low to minimum effectiveness band, what might it cost your facility if there were a complaint or planned inspection and subsequent fines issued? How do those fines counterbalance with costs of upgrades to 100% compliance? What might it cost your facility to move around staffing to accommodate an employee who is out for post-exposure prophylaxis (this is extremely important in smaller practices as there are many fewer people to step in to cover shifts)?

Status Quo Analysis

Is what you have now enough? Are you in compliance? Some occupational health programs are in remarkably good shape or have such great systems in place already that they see very few cases of occupational infectious disease. If this is the case (and boy do we all wish it was for us), identify if you want to do more. Is the hospital in great shape, but the affiliated outpatient locations, not so much? Does the success of your program warrant building others to mirror it?

Can you work with infection prevention and control and have them learn from you? Can you provide additional value to the broader facility or system or community? If it is any of these things, what would funding look like? What metrics would you create to propose expansion to leadership? What might cost of acquiring new technologies or additional PPE cost?

Warp Speed Ahead Maximum Effectiveness Analysis

You may be rolling your eyes at this one, but many healthcare systems are taking safety so seriously that they are funding improving infrastructure like crazy. If this is the case, you want to be ready with your charts and graphs and ask in hand when the money is being passed around because this may be the most taxing category of all because it requires changing leaderships' perception.

Occupational infection prevention programs are seen as "the cost of doing business" or a non-revenue-generating department. You can prove them wrong. When the operating room (OR) is putting together their financial plans for acquiring the latest and greatest robot to drive in high end surgical patients, you are competing directly with them.

The best laid occupational health plans are ones that contribute directly as recruiting and retention programs for the best and brightest workers. What is the potential value of driving home messaging in the community as "the safest place to work"? How might that make your facility much more desirable to clinical training programs and bringing in additional funding? If your facility has magnet designation, how might improving on already terrific programs increase marketability to attract new patients and clinical talent?

Whatever the category you are in or if several different departments or locations straddle across one or two, you have to think like a business person, not just a technical person. Here are some tools that can help putting together some numbers or statistics to build your financial "portfolio."

Original 1999 calculations (Source: Kohn and Ferry, 1999) were adjusted for cost of living and inflation, multiplied by factor of 1.5 (approximately 150%). For example, $100 in 1999 is more like $150 in 2020

A chart like Table 8.1 can help to estimate cost associated with a specific risk, department to department. For example, a direct exposure to Ebola can result in a

Table 8.1 Measuring magnitudes of severity of consequences

Magnitude	Cost, loss, or liability ($)	Effects on workers	Effects on public	Effects on environment
7	$15,000,000	Fatality or permanent health effect (e.g., Ebola)	Fatality of permanent health effect	Widespread and long term or permanent
6	$1500,000	Fatality or permanent health effect (e.g., HCV source positive needlestick)	Severe or multiple injuries	Widespread and short term or localized and long term
5	$150,000	Severe or multiple illnesses (e.g., measles outbreak or MRSA infection)	Injury, illness, or hospitalization	Widespread and short term or localized and long term
4	$15,000	Lost workday(s) (e.g., source negative needlestick or splash)	Impact on direct contacts (spouse, partner, household)	Localized, short or long term
3	$1500	Medical treatment (e.g., eye splash with non-blood contaminated saliva)	Likely none	Likely none
2	$150	First-aid case (e.g., cut with clean scalpel blade)	Likely none	Likely none
1	No exposure incident			

fatality in a facility where research is done, as it was in Dallas, Texas, in 2014. This may not happen all that frequently, but when it does the cost is high.

On a nursing unit with high-risk HIV patients, a needlestick can result in seroconversion to not just HIV, but based on what we know about co-infections, to HBV, HCV, or others. These may cost less, but the likelihood of frequency is much higher. It is best here to be as specific as possible to include this as part of an exposure or hazard assessment. It serves double duty as both building risk assessment plans and building out financial value/risk.

A simple way to determine the most accurate estimates is to do an equation that may look something like this:

$$\text{Frequency / Incidence} \times \text{Cost} = \text{Risk}$$

If it is known that there were 40 needlesticks in the OR last year, that may translate to 40 x (range from $1500,000 to $150) = $60,000,000 to $6000. This is a huge hypothetical range, but it goes to show that the cost of purchasing, using, activating, and immediately disposing of safer medical devices can save the facility potentially millions of dollars. That said, it is crucial to work with materials management and supply chain and counterbalance these costs with the cost of devices (or the cost difference moving from non-safety to safety).

Calculating a "Return on Investment" (ROI) may or may not translate well depending on the facility type and size. Traditional ROI calculations are estimated by the following equation:

$$ROI = Total\ Estimated\ Benefit\ /\ Total\ Cost\ of\ Goods\ \&\ Services$$

In an occupational infection prevention and control program, this is incredibly difficult to do for the program as a whole because the benefits and costs are not clear cut. It may be a more useful tool as a companion to the risk determinations above performed on a department by department or procedure by procedure basis.

For example, it is difficult to determine what the actual benefit is for instituting universal eye protection for every clinical employee and what it would cost (acquisition, replacement, loss/theft, etc.), but if eye exposures are occurring most frequently in patient and exam rooms, it may be more straightforward to estimate what those exposures have or might cost and what the price (or cost) of putting in eyewear caddies in rooms or on doors might be. The manufacturers, vendors, and/or distributors would be more than happy to assist you with these calculations and help build the business case.

In closing, this must be said – facilities are required to comply with OSHA and all other federal standards, so cost cannot be a reason *not* to comply, rather it becomes useful to expand compliance into the maximum effectiveness realm or if there is head to head competition with another department on the impact of funding. The finance department will very likely have budget planning forms with the ability to estimate and analyze work power, equipment lists, materials, and other costs. Also, if there is a great deal further to go and need additional staff, identifying the right skill level and associated salary is a must. Must this be done in house or should a consultant/contractor be hired? Between finance, accounting, and human resources, there should be plenty of colleagues that can help.

While this guide is not focused on building an operational culture of safety, it does provide resources for getting you started or for laying a more solid foundation. Building your facility-wide institutional culture of safety is not going to be up to one person or one department, and it certainly is not going to be up to you. A culture is cultivated over time, across experiences, and has its successes, failures, upticks, and downturns.

Here are some of the tools needed to plant the seeds of a culture from within a healthcare environment. The resources are intended to help along the journey as you "teach up".

Example 1
Your facility is adding new single occupancy patient rooms, and your leadership teams have shared the initial schematics with your department, but you don't see any clear space for storing or placing PPE like gloves, gowns, or eye protection. There may be wall space to screw in mounted exam glove caddies, but other than limited sink space, there is no room for anything else.

Since we know that improving accessibility of PPE is key to improving compliance and protection, it is important that you take this as a Teaching Up

Opportunity. Sort through the exposure data that you have on eye splashes and put together some simple graphs or charts and use those to teach your management and/or leadership about what occupational exposures are occurring and how important it is to have space built in for in-room eye protection storage. If you have information on how much these exposures cost the facility in post-exposure medical follow-up and sorting through staffing issues, share that too. *[If your surveillance system does not capture details about how the exposure happened and if the employee was wearing eye protection when it did – expand your system – there are free systems out there that are easy to download, like International Safety Center's Exposure Prevention Information Network (EPINet®).]*

Space is a premium investment in health care; you may be competing with other clinical areas to justify space needed to protect staff from occupational exposure to infectious disease, so you may need to fight for it. The best fights can be won by evidence-based teaching moments.

Example 2

The nurses' station and surrounding area are constantly visited by patients, families, visitors, and other clinical colleagues. Everyone puts their hands and arms up on the counter as they talk and wait. This countertop surface becomes contaminated with touch contaminants like MRSA, VRE, cold, flu, and more. As staff touch and move about and visitors touch and move about, this surface has now become a vector for microbial acquisition and transmission. Other than daily surface cleaning and disinfection from environmental services (EVS), there is no other active process in place for common or public area cleaning.

Transmission can be devastating especially to immunocompromised patients with indwelling catheters, and it is most likely that microbes are transmitted via hands and contaminated clothing or uniforms (scrubs, lab coats) if hand hygiene and PPE use is less than optimal.

This is an easy and important, high-impact Teaching Up Opportunity. Create a poster, infographic, or cartoon that describes how microbes are transmitted and how long they thrive on surfaces. Post it at the nurses' station next to popup, disposable surface wipes. Put alcohol-based hand rubs on the counter for anyone who visits to use. Remind unit staff and any colleagues (and their managing supervisors) visiting from other departments that while surface contamination and cross-transmission to patients is the most risky, staff (especially during flu season or during other types of outbreaks) do not want to get themselves or their families sick either.

This may take convincing the unit nurse managers who are so focused on making sure that patients are cared for and staffing is adequate that they may forget about little, important details like these. They will thank you for protecting their staff and their patients.

Tools and Resources
Free, All Access Programs and Checklists
- CDC. Pandemic Flu Checklist for Workplace Administrators: https://www.cdc.gov/nonpharmaceutical-interventions/pdf/pan-flu-checklist-workplace-administrators-item1.pdf
- CDC. Workplace Administrators: Flu Prevention at Work (Non-Pharmaceutical Interventions) https://www.cdc.gov/nonpharmaceutical-interventions/workplace/workplace-administrators.html
- CDC. Worksite Health Scorecard. https://www.cdc.gov/workplacehealth-promotion/initiatives/healthscorecard/index.html
- OSHA. Employer Guidance Reducing All Workers' Exposures to Seasonal Flu Virus https://www.osha.gov/dts/guidance/flu/nonhealthcare.html
- Otter J. Counting the Cost of Contact Precautions. https://reflectionsipc.com/2018/03/07/counting-the-cost-of-contact-precautions/

Free, All Access Presentation
- The Influence of Safety Culture and Climate on Compliance with PPE (Institute of Medicine, Gershon) http://www.nationalacademies.org/hmd/~/media/Files/Activity%20Files/PublicHealth/FluPersProtEquip/Gershon.pdf

Posters
- CDC. Don't Spread Germs at Work Poster. https://www.cdc.gov/nonpharmaceutical-interventions/pdf/dont-spread-germs-work-employers-item2.pdf
- CDC. Stay Home if You're Sick Poster. https://www.cdc.gov/nonpharmaceutical-interventions/pdf/stay-home-youre-sick-employers-item4.pdf
- CDC.
- Everyday Preventive Actions Can Help Fight Germs, Like Flu. https://www.cdc.gov/flu/pdf/freeresources/updated/everyday-preventive-actions-8.5x11.pdf

Educational Curricula
- Culture of Safety. (Patient Safety Primer, same principles hold true for Worker Safety) https://psnet.ahrq.gov/primers/primer/5
- Develop a Culture of Safety (Institute for Healthcare Improvement, also built with patient safety in mind, but all principles hold true for worker safety) http://www.ihi.org/resources/Pages/Changes/DevelopaCultureofSafety.aspx

Building Incentive Programs
- Participant Engagement and The Use of Incentives Consideration. (Part of CDC Work Place Health Resource Center) https://www.cdc.gov/workplacehealthpromotion/initiatives/resource-center/index.html
- Resource for Building Economic and Cost Analyses
- Kohn JP and Ferry TS. Safety and Health Management Planning. Government Institutes. 1999.

References

Bureau of Labor Statistics. (2019). *Distribution of nonfatal occupational injuries and illnesses by private industry sector, 2018*. https://www.bls.gov/iif/soii-chart-data-2018.htm

Crum, A. J., & Langer, E. J. (2007). Mind-set matters: Exercise and the placebo effect. *Psychological Science, 18*(2), 165–171.

Efstathiou, G., et al. (2011). Factors influencing nurses' compliance with standard precautions in order to avoid occupational exposure to microorganisms: A focus group study. *BMC Nursing, 10*, 1.

Grosch, J. W., et al. (1999). Safety climate dimensions associated with occupational exposure to blood-borne pathogens in nurses. *American Journal of Industrial Medicine, Suppl 1*, 122–124.

International Safety Center. (2018). *Summary reports for needlestick and sharp object injuries and blood and body fluid exposures*. www.internationalsafetycenter.org/reports

Kohn, J. P., & Ferry, T. S. (1999). *Safety and health management planning*. Government Institutes. Rockville, MD, USA.

Lally, P., van Jaarsveld, C. H., Potts, H. W., & Wardle, J. (2010). How are habits formed: Modelling habit formation in the real world. *European Journal of Social Psychology, 40*, 998–1009.

Lakhiani, V. (2016). *The code of the extraordinary mind: 10 unconventional Laws to redefine your life and succeed on your own terms*. Rodale Books.

OSHA. (2020). OSHA Penalties. https://www.osha.gov/penalties.

Chapter 9
Engineering Controls and Safer Medical Devices

Objectives
- Identify the role of engineering controls in the hierarchy of controls.
- Introduce the role that adjunct or adjuvant technologies can play in reducing environmental pathogens.
- Summarize engineering controls for safer options for medical devices, textiles, and antimicrobial technologies.

The American Industrial Hygiene Association (AIHA) defines an engineering control as "process change, substitution, isolation, ventilation, source modification." This is a rather broad definition and takes into account all types of health hazards including chemical, radiation, dust, biological, and more (AIHA 1997).

We know that the OSHA Bloodborne Pathogens Standard uses a definition more specific to biological hazards: "controls (e.g., sharps disposal containers, self-sheathing needles, safer medical devices, such as sharps with engineered sharps injury protections and needleless systems) that isolate or remove the bloodborne pathogens hazard from the workplace" (OSHA 1991, 2001).

Relative to occupational exposure to infectious disease, a combination of the two might be most appropriate. Let's be bold enough to set a new definition for this unique hazard in health care here:

Engineering Controls isolate or remove exposures to pathogenic microorganisms using physical means including ventilation, safer medical devices, and containment.

This definition more appropriately considers its specific location in the hierarchy of controls and hones in on physical controls that are engineered for protecting workers from infectious disease risks. For microorganisms, the AIHA definition includes controls that are already addressed by the hierarchy including substitution

© Springer Nature Switzerland AG 2020
A. H. Mitchell, *Preventing Occupational Exposures to Infectious Disease in Health Care*, https://doi.org/10.1007/978-3-030-56039-3_9

and administrative controls (process change). It also telescopes out and incorporates more than just medical devices with engineered features that reduce needlesticks and sharps injuries.

Let's get started on each individual element of this new definition and the role they play in protecting personnel (and patients) from exposure to pathogenic microorganisms.

Ventilation

Ventilation isolates infectious hazards by means of air movement and filtration. This includes ventilation from the outside in, the inside out, and the inside throughout (Fig. 9.1). It is done through regulating air changes per hour, positive and negative pressure, and air filtration like HEPA filters in HVAC systems. Also it includes localized areas like biological safety cabinets and fume hoods, as well as instrumentation that generates gas and vapor.

The selection of filter type depends on the potential hazard. Since bacteria, viruses, fungi, and spores are different sizes, the type of filtration selected must match the hazards likely in the specific area or department of interest.

According to the Cal OSHA Aerosol Transmissible Disease Standard (§5199), the following definition is in place for negative pressure (CalOSHA 2009). For infectious diseases, the concept is to keep the pathogen inside the patient room or laboratory and not to have it vent outward:

> Negative pressure. A relative air pressure difference between two adjacent areas. The atmospheric pressure in a containment room or area that is under negative pressure is lower than adjacent areas, which keeps air from flowing out of the containment facility and into adjacent rooms or areas preventing the outward spread of the contaminant.

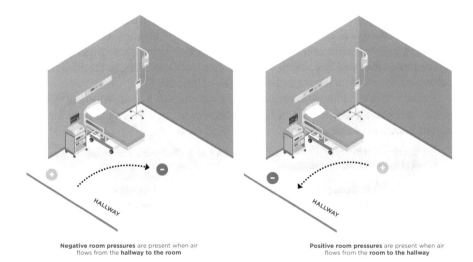

Negative room pressures are present when air
flows from the hallway to the room

Positive room pressures are present when air
flows from the room to the hallway

Fig. 9.1 Negative and positive pressure patient rooms (Chelsey Armstrong (artist), 2020)

On the contrary, positive pressure is used on nearly all other rooms in a health-care setting where immunocompromised patients are so that the air flows out of the room to keep microorganisms and other contaminants off or away from the patient. Think of it as lifting the bugs off and away. The reason this is not acceptable for people with known infectious diseases like TB or COVID-19, for example, is because the idea is to keep that patient "isolated" so their air does not become a potential hazard to anyone sharing that ventilation pathway in the next room or down the hall or wherever the air "exhausts."

An easy way to remember which is good for which is positive for patients, but negative for nuclei (microorganisms).

Room air exchanges are an important element of overall ventilation engineering controls. Typically, healthcare facilities have 10 air changes per hour (ACH), but for extremely immunocompromised patients like those having just undergone an organ transplant, they can be as frequent as 30. The industrial hygienist in partnership with infection prevention and environmental health and safety in your facility will know precisely what flow is safest.

ASHRAE offers mandatory minimum requirements for "Ventilation of Health Care Facilities" in its ANSI/ASHRAE/ASHE Standard 170–2013 (ASHRAE 1999, 2013). Healthcare and medical facilities planners, including architects, HVAC engineers, and facilities management, identify that poorly ventilated healthcare facilities can result in increased circulation of mold, spores, and other pathogens that can cause infection, illness, or allergic reactions in workers, patients, and visitors.

Spores, Mold, and Construction Remediation

There are no standards or occupational exposure limits established for mold and spores; therefore, it's important that internal processes and policies are set by each facility depending on geographic location (humidity, rainfall), new or ongoing construction projects for rebuilds/renovations, and remediation after natural disasters like hurricanes. The extent to which mold spores cause human illness is relatively unknown. Those with compromised immune or respiratory systems and asthma should limit exposures as symptoms such as nasal stuffiness, eye irritation, wheezing, or skin irritation can be extreme in populations with other underlying respiratory conditions.

The greatest risk is to patients. Workers with known mold allergies need also to be careful to limit potential exposure, as should those responsible for cleaning up and remediation including environmental services (EVS), housekeeping, construction, and remediation crews.

Before any cleanup begins, the extent of the mold growth and the water source feeding its growth must be determined. Once the extent of growth and source are determined, the first step is to stop the water intrusion as mold growth will continue until the water source is removed. Once the water intrusion is stopped, an inventory of damage must be made. All permeable material that has been damaged should be replaced. This included upholstered furniture and wall partitions and wall board. Due to its wicking properties, wall board should be scored and removed 18 inches above the highest water level.

When performing clean up, rubber boots, rubber gloves, goggles, and respiratory protection should be worn according to CDC. In order to avoid mouth and nose exposures, faceshields and/or respirators should be worn. When respirators are used, a respiratory protection program must be in place. OSHA provides guidance for mold remediation as well as disposal. A resource list is provided at the end of this chapter.

Since detergents and bleach are frequently used for remediation of impermeable materials, it is important to keep inhalation and skin contact at bay and consider the most appropriate PPE and controls for eliminating both exposure to spores and cleaners and disinfectants.

Air and Surface Disinfection

Ultraviolet Technology

In the last 10 years, there has been an onslaught of technologies that are designed to disinfect the air and the physical healthcare environment using "robots" that emit ultraviolet (UV), ozone, or hydrogen peroxide. These devices can range in size from a coffee maker to a dishwasher to a large, upright water heater.

They are intended to be used in conjunction with regular manual surface cleaning and disinfection performed by either nursing or EVS staff. There is unfortunately great variation in how patient, exam, procedure, and operating rooms are serviced (cleaned and disinfected) between patients and during terminal cleans (after a patient with known infectious disease has been discharged/transferred). The Association for the Health Care Environment (AHE) has resources, guidance, and publications for room cleaning and disinfection.

UV has been used for decades as disinfection for water. It is an effective microcidal agent, and depending on the intended purpose for it in your facility, the positioning and cycle time will vary. Shortwave UV-C is typically used for the disinfection of medical devices in healthcare settings. There is an ever-growing number of manufacturers and suppliers of UV technology. Machines are mobile and easy to use and can be programmed for varying cycle times. There has been a growing body of evidence that they are effective in reducing pathogens that cause infection in patients, but less is known about their ability to prevent illness and infection in workers.

The downfall of UV technologies is that they are "line-of-sight" killers, meaning if it is being used in a room with a ton of equipment, furniture, or patient care items, it will not be effective (on one cycle) around corners or in nooks and crannies. Some facilities use metallic paints to overcome this issue. Also depending on the surfaces in a room – plastic, vinyl, cloth, stainless steel, composites, etc. – UV may affect each surface over the medium to longer term differently. Think of it similarly to cracking and sun damaged lawn furniture. Increased damage may mean that microbes could survive even longer in cracks and crevices. It would help greatly to ask any potential vendor, manufacturer, or distributor about surface compatibility and published studies prior to considering this method. That goes with any method as the last thing a facility would want to do is damage surfaces and increase microbial growth *because of* the method selected.

UV's effectiveness also depends on the amount and type of bioburden or contamination on a surface, as well as wavelength being used, humidity, and other factors. Just as it is unsafe to be in the sun for an extended period of time, it is important to be careful about any occupational exposures to UV from these machines. They are also powered by electricity, so any safety precautions put in place for electrical and cord tripping hazards must also be implemented when using these types of mobile disinfection technologies.

There need to be occupational health and safety precautions put into place when using UV technology, and since the FDA currently does not regulate these types of machines, it is important to follow the manufacturers' instructions for use. Most machines require that no person is inside the room during use and that the door is closed.

Hydrogen Peroxide

In an effort to overcome the issue with line-of-sight UV technologies, hydrogen peroxide "foggers" have emerged on the market. These robot-like machines can be rolled into a room and emit vaporized hydrogen peroxide for a set time period. Hydrogen peroxide (H_2O_2) is relatively safe in that it is used in hundreds of products to clean and/or lighten teeth, skin, linen, surfaces, and more.

Hydrogen peroxide is an extremely effective disinfectant and sterilant. It is used to sterilize surgical and medical devices in sterile processing and central supply departments of hospitals. The difficulties with H_2O_2 however include execution of the fogging process in a room. There are requirements to seal off air registers, seal the underside of doors, and remove bed linen, paper products, and more. Because there are several steps to prepare a room for "fogging," time is an issue. Also unlike UV, H_2O_2 exposure is regulated by OSHA. A facility must have and follow safety controls indicated on the safety data sheet and have air sampling protocols in place.

The OSHA PEL and NIOSH REL are both 1 ppm. Hydrogen peroxide is a known occupational irritant, and as such there are strict regulations in place for use of PPE during potential H_2O_2 exposures. If you choose to implement hydrogen peroxide technologies in your facility as an adjunct to infection prevention and surface disinfection, be sure to provide occupational health and safety input to whatever applicable committee is determining purchasing and implementation decisions.

Ozone

Ozone has also been used for years to disinfect drinking water and now has application for disinfection and sterilization in health care. This type of technology is typically used in chambers to process medical and surgical devices, but can also be used in rooms. CDC HICPAC provides background and guidance on ozone use. This is not as frequently used as other technologies, but if you are interested in considering it for use in reducing either patient or worker exposures to infectious disease, there are several resources provided at the end of this chapter.

Device Cleaning, Disinfection, and Sterilization

Most critical or semi-critical medical devices are cleaned and processed in a stand-alone department – sterile processing department (SPD) or central sterile supply department (CSSD). These reusable medical devices are frequently used for endoscopy and surgical procedures.

Though the devices are cleaned and either disinfected (semi-critical) or sterilized (critical) to protect patients from residual pathogenic organisms, workers can also be exposed to them especially during the reprocessing step itself. Cleaning endoscopes, for example, require a great deal of manual cleaning, brushing, flushing, and rinsing (if not using an Endoscope Cleaner and Reprocessor [ECR] or Automated Endoscope Cleaner and Reprocessor [AER]).

During these required steps, blood and body fluids can be aerated. Disinfectants used for scope and device reprocessing include glutaraldehyde, ortho-phthalaldehyde (OPA), and peracetic acid. These chemicals have their own individual occupational exposure hazards, and CDC, NIOSH, and OSHA all have resources and references in place to prevent risks that can cause injury or illness.

It is therefore critically important that whoever is reprocessing medical devices is protected from not only the body fluids and pathogenic organisms but also the chemicals used as detergents and disinfectants. Not only are there biological and chemical hazards associated with these job tasks but also physical – including repetitive motion, lifting, torqueing, and reaching.

During the initial cleaning/rinsing process (gross decontamination), there is also potential dangers from a very wet environment, so slips and falls are highly likely. Nonslip flooring and footwear should be considered as well as the institution of administrative controls – such as alternating tasks throughout the SPD or CSSD. For example, it could look like this: 1 hour on decontamination, break, 1 hour on pre-processing wrapping and packaging, break, 1 hour on sterilization machinery, etc.

Ideally, all device reprocessing should be done using as much automation as possible to protect workers from exposures, as well as to maintain consistency. Automated machines also have chemical and biological indicators as part of their systematic "anatomy" to ensure that levels are sufficient enough to kill and to stay killed.

Machines that are used to reprocess medical devices include different types of chemical and physical hazards. Steam and hydrogen peroxide are most frequently used now, but ethylene oxide (EtO) still exists in healthcare settings for devices that cannot otherwise be sterilized. Steam has clear physical hazards like heat/burns and water/slips. Hydrogen peroxide as discussed above can be a hazard if there is leakage from a sterilizer. Ethylene oxide is extremely hazardous, and it should be phased out of your facility or potentially managed by a dedicated third party. There have been several very public lawsuits about the impact of EtO in the environment and among members of the communities that live near EtO processing facilities. Unfortunately, until there is better or different technology to sterilize consumer and patient care items like sterile gauze or sterile gloves, we are stuck with it and must do as much as possible to contain any hazards.

There is an entire profession dedicated to reprocessing medical devices and a couple of professional organizations focused on making these processes safe. They are your best, comprehensive reference and include resources and tools from the International Association of Healthcare Central Service Materiel Management (IAHCSMM).

Safer Medical Devices

Not all pathogenic microorganisms circulate in the air and can be "captured" with localized ventilation. Since the patient or specimen is a potential harbor for blood-borne or infectious disease, there must also be protections and controls put into place at the source. Here, the reliance safer medical devices and instruments are most appropriate. Since these are required to be used per the OSHA Bloodborne Pathogens Standard, their implementation is it only a safest practice, but also required by law (US federal regulations).

Safer medical devices can come in many forms. At their base, they are devices that have some degree of safety feature engineered into them to protect not only the user but anyone downstream that may encounter a contaminated device on a surface, in the trash or dirty linen, or poking out of an overfilled sharps container (i.e., environmental services, housekeeping, waste haulers, laundry personnel, etc.). They are engineering controls.

Some examples include:

- Needles on syringes, intravenous (IV) catheters, IV access, and blood or specimen collection devices that have built-in or add-on mechanisms that isolate sharp after use
- Skin closure devices, techniques, or adhesives that eliminate the use of sharp tip sutures
- Scalpels, and other surgical devices, that eliminate, sheath, or protect the sharp
- Closed system transfer devices for blood, body fluids, or hazardous drugs
- Physical barriers that redirect potential exposures at the source (e.g., suction, wound irrigation)

- Closed suction canisters
- Engineered or technical textiles or surfaces worn as uniforms or used for upholstery, patient care items, or environmental surfaces

Most attention has been placed on safer medical devices that protect employees
from a needle or sharp – sharps injury prevention (SIP) devices (Fig. 9.2). These
include disposable syringes, IV or central line catheters, anesthesia needles, lancets,
pen needles, blades/scalpels, sutures, blood collection devices, and more that have
a retracting or blunt/blunted needle or a needle that is protected by a hinged arm or
sliding sheath.

New engineering controls are coming on the market every year to protect users
against splash and splatter of blood and body fluids immediately at the source
(patient). The benefit of these types of engineering controls is that in situations
where hazardous drugs are also being used (chemotherapy, antineoplastics, hor-
mones, etc.), they also work to protect personnel from exposure to these chemical
hazards.

Where withdrawing medications from vials or ampoules is a common practice
(insulin, vaccination programs, agriculture, etc.), there are also engineering designs
for mounted holders that allow for a one-handed technique. These controls reduce

Fig. 9.2 Examples of safer medical devices: sharps injury prevention features (CDC 2008)

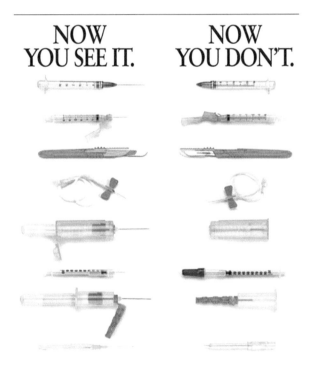

NOW
YOU SEE IT.

NOW
YOU DON'T.

PROTECT YOURSELF AND OTHERS-
USE SHARPS WITH SAFETY FEATURES

awkwardness in drawing up medications that can result in a sharps injury or an error in dosing. There are also controls for dentistry that eliminate injuries from recapping multi-dosing dental dispensing devices. These devices again can work overtime and protect patient and personnel.

Finally, the hierarchy of controls demands that where sharps can be altogether eliminated they should be. For example, this includes using a blunt fill needle for medication preparation (e.g., reconstituting medications in a vial) or a blood transfer device when drawing up blood or specimens using a syringe into a vacuum tube. If medications, vaccinations, or other therapeutics come in a glass ampule, not only should blunt fill needles be used but blunt fill needles with filters so that glass particulates are not inadvertently transferred from the ampule to the patient. Many vaccine manufacturers are moving toward pre-filled syringes with sharps injury prevention needles attached. This is for safety of both patient/receiver and worker/provider.

Since suture needles make up a large percentage of sharps injuries reported year after year, there should be considerations for eliminating them where possible (EPINet 2019). This could be true with innovations in skin closure, including the use of adhesives or zipper closures.

An additional resource for evaluation and selection of sharps injury prevention devices is the Training for Development of Innovative Control Technologies (TDICT) Project Safer Medical Device Evaluation Forms available at www.tdict.org.

Device Evaluation Forms are available for:

- Scalpels and blades
- Safer injection
- Vascular access devices
- Needleless IV connectors
- Blood collection systems
- Protective eyewear
- Gloves
- Sharps containers
- Devices used in dentistry

Passive and Active Devices

Engineering control features for medical devices can be both active and passive. Active devices require the user to do something to activate the safety mechanism. Active features can be activated by a single hand, finger, or hard surface (table top) depending on the type. They can be in the form of a simple push button or more complex second hand activation and locking action (think barrel-like sliding sheath).

Most retracting needle devices require the user to depress the plunger of a disposable hypodermic syringe deeper (beyond) the depth required to administer all the medication in the barrel of the syringe. The drawn-up medication, vaccine, or therapeutic is administered in its whole dose, and then the plunger needs to be depressed a smidge more to activate the needle retracting feature.

Depending on what the device is used for and the comfort level and mastery of the user, selection of a single-handed activation may be safer as to prevent the introduction of a second hand into the field of risk (near the tip of the contaminated needle). This decision should be addressed during device evaluation.

This is not unlike "childproofing." Over-the-counter and prescription drug bottles nearly always require the consumer/user to actively childproof an aspirin container, for example, by actively pressing and turning the lid to open. Then the consumer/user must make sure the lid clicks in place upon closing to create a harder to open container when and if children encounter it.

These devices, containers, and bottles are active. The user must actively do something to ensure its safety.

The OSHA Bloodborne Pathogens Standard requires that not only must employers (regulated facilities) implement the use of safety engineered or safer medical (sharps injury prevention) devices (Fig. 9.3), but also as a requirement of the 2000 Needlestick Safety and Prevention Act that nonmanagerial frontline employees be a part of device evaluation and selection. Devices selected must be appropriate for the procedures being performed and may not be selected purely based on price or group purchasing contracts. OSHA has several letters of interpretation on these issues available on their website (https://www.osha.gov/pls/oshaweb/owasrch. search_form?p_doc_type=INTERPRETATIONS&p_toc_level=3&p_keyvalue=1910.1030&p_status=CURRENT).

As illustrated in the list of examples above, safer devices are to protect users not only from injuries from needles but also from non-hollow bore solid sharps like blades on scalpels, sutures, screws and pins, broken glass, and even bone shards in orthopedic or emergency trauma cases. There are engineering controls for these devices including scalpels with retractable sheaths, blunt sutures for internal fascia (non-skin closure), skin adhesives, "zipper"-type skin closures, and more. This device field is constantly changing and innovating as patients demand less invasive surgeries with better, faster surgical recovery times and in nonhospital locations like ambulatory or outpatient surgery settings.

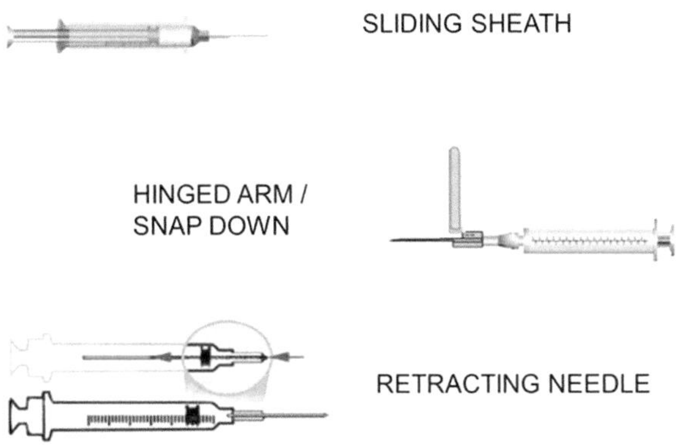

Fig. 9.3 Example Devices with Safety Features (OSHA 2001, OSHA n.d.)

SLIDING SHEATH

HINGED ARM / SNAP DOWN

RETRACTING NEEDLE

In some cases, there is no needle or sharp at all, but an engineering control or safer medical device that protects the user from a splash or splatter of blood or body fluid. This can include products like closed suction canisters, wound irrigation syringes with physical splash guards, and more.

The employer is required to keep up with changing technologies and commercially available safer medical devices and must review them at least annually (or as they become available). The market for engineering controls is building and expanding far quicker than for PPE, and the choices can be overwhelming.

This is where you come in. You can assist in the communication of the availability of these types of devices in your institution and throughout your professional network. A great resource for staying abreast of innovations are email listservs (like MCOH-EH: https://mylist.net/listinfo/mcoh-eh), vendors, distributors, and many of the others listed at the end of this chapter.

Technical Textiles

Uniforms

Just as environmental and high-touch surfaces in health care become contaminated and can serve as reservoirs and vectors for acquisition and transmission of pathogens, so can textiles. These include bed linen, privacy curtains, patient gowns, practitioner's clothing, and uniforms (including scrubs and lab coats). Textiles and woven fabrics are sometimes better at retaining organisms because they are porous and "sticky," so cells can take hold and hitchhike their way through healthcare facilities and even communities.

It is indisputable that uniforms are contaminated during work shifts. One can argue that this is true no matter the work that is being performed. Depending on laundering practice and personal hygiene, uniforms can be contaminated even at the beginning of a work shift (Burden et al. 2011; Fijan and Turk 2012; Mitchell et al. 2015).

If PPE including isolation gowns are not donned and/or doffed at the appropriate time, this increases the likelihood that uniforms will continue to be a source of contamination, not only for patient exposure to pathogens but also to co-workers and colleagues and anyone coming into contact with that person wearing that garment. Until it is removed, anyone in its path can be unintentionally exposed, including commuters on a public transportation, kids being picked up from daycare, fellow shoppers at the grocery store, and families at home.

How many times have you seen a person in scrubs shopping for produce or at your local coffee shop? Hundreds, right?

As onlookers, we have no idea if they are a medical transcriptionist working in an office setting, a pharmaceutical sales rep, a dental hygienist, a critical care nurse, a scrub/uniform salesperson, or an orthopedic surgeon working in the operating room. Each level of work task will result in varying levels of potential contamination. Most surgeons will doff all PPE prior to leaving a healthcare facility and return into their normal street clothes, but this is not always the case.

The United States seems to be the only country that does not require all healthcare personnel wearing scrubs and lab coats to leave them behind at their workplace. Rather, people wear them around like badge of honor. We must stop this practice if we are to safely reduce transmission of pathogens out in the community and home to our elderly parents or young kids.

To compensate for subpar uniform wearing practices, several manufacturers have developed textiles with engineered properties that are either fluid repellent or antimicrobial or both. Since there is frequent exposure to blood and body fluids that splash or splatter on to uniforms, the fluid repellency is ideal of reducing physical, gross contamination so that the antimicrobial can work effectively on whatever contamination is left behind. Textiles that are antimicrobial only may have a very difficult time killing anything more than a fine, microscopic layer of bacteria. As such, several studies have recognized that antimicrobial scrubs or textiles alone may not be effective in its protective ability to patient nor care provider.

Technologies like these are rapidly becoming available for all kinds of worn textiles as well as fabric treatments for upholstery. If your facility is considering any of these types of textile technologies, be sure that you have considered what type of antimicrobial or fluid repellency chemicals they have been treated with so that best and safest decisions can be made for preventing potential leaching and skin irritation/allergies and maintaining best properties during laundering.

An important note regarding OSHA compliance for scrubs: If scrubs are worn as PPE, the employer is required to provide them to employees at no cost as well as pay for replacement garments and laundering. Many operating room and surgical personnel wear scrubs as PPE and gain access to them through scrubs "vending machines" or through sterile supply.

If scrubs are worn as a uniform – meaning they are not provided as workplace/employer-based gowns, aprons, and coveralls that function as PPE – this would not be the case. Employers would not be required to provide, replace, and launder them.

If scrubs purchased and worn by clinical or support staff become contaminated at work –soiled with blood or body fluids – they must be removed and properly containerized in a clearly labeled or red bag.

Technically, it is safest that the employer launder those garments to protect the worker wearing them and the families or communities that may come into contact with them. But, if that is not the case (which it unfortunately often isn't), there needs to be a process in place for safe containment (bagging and tagging/labeling). This is so that anyone potentially coming into contact with them downstream is appropriately protected. The reason why this is not often the case is because it is too logistically difficult and fiscally prohibitive for employers to launder employee-purchased and provided scrubs:

> How would they be handled by massive washers and dryers? How would they be labeled and returned to the employee? What if laundry is being done outside of the facility? How is this handled? You get the point – it gets complicated.

It is one of the reasons that OSHA only covers employee safety and health and the provisions associated with providing and laundering PPE and not uniforms. However, your facility may want to have a process in place that protects all potential points of contact. What is your process/procedure for managing employee-purchased uniforms? What do you require them to do? Should they really be bringing them home to launder when their families, friends, and communities could be exposed to the contaminants on them?

Make sure you have a program in place in your facility that takes these elements into account and provides the safest possible "worn" environment for your personnel.

CDC does recommend that for any linen/laundry that is "infected" it be washed at a very high temperature (160 F) and that bleach (50–150 ppm) be added. Most home washing machines cannot get this hot because of child scalding laws, and many manufacturers of brightly colored scrubs will warn the purchaser not to use bleach to protect the dye used for coloring; be mindful of both of these elements when putting your plans and processes together.

Laundry

It is not only the linen and textiles themselves that pose direct risk to patients and personnel coming in contact to them in patient, procedure, and exam rooms but also the EVS, laundry, and linen workers processing used, contaminated linen. There have been documented outbreaks around the world for illness and infection caused by contaminated laundry (HICPAC 2008; Fijan and Turk 2012; Mitchell 2015).

And this risk can ring true for the person removing linen, privacy curtains, or patient gowns after they have been used. It can be true for the person transporting linen or sorting and washing linen. It can also be true – depending on how effective the washing and drying process is – to those after who may be handling washed and dried, but still contaminated textiles.

CDC, HLAC, and several other organizations have recommendations for safe handling of contaminated linen as well as proper washing and drying protocols including water temperature, use of detergents and bleach, and dry time and temperature. We know that since inappropriate disposal of contaminated sharps is still a problem resulting in downstream needlestick injuries, it is important to consider how laundry bagging and sorting is being down to prevent these types of inadvertent injuries. Many facilities use some form of puncture-resistant gloves when doing sorting.

Contaminants can be airborne during transport and sorting, so consider what PPE may be appropriate for these types of exposures. This can be especially true for infectious disease that is easily aerated and can live in comfy little moist pockets like TB. Laundry facilities (whether in-house or third party/contract) can be hot and wet and crowded. They are typically unpleasant work environments, so you may also want to include safety controls for hazards like heat, burns, slips, lifting, and repetitive motion.

Providing the safest possible environment to protect personnel from occupational exposure to infectious disease in health care may seem incredibly daunting. There are terrific tools, resources, and references to help you develop, revamp, or revise your in-house programs, processes, procedures, and policies. You do not need to reinvent the wheel relative to evaluating new and existing engineering controls and safer medical devices.

Tools and Resources
- AHE Knowledge Center. http://www.ahe.org/knowledge-center/
- ASHRAE Health Care Facilities Resources. https://www.ashrae.org/resources%2D%2Dpublications/bookstore/health-care-facilities-resources
- CDC HICPAC Guidelines for Environmental Infection Control in Health Care. https://www.cdc.gov/infectioncontrol/pdf/guidelines/environmental-guidelines.pdf
- CDC HICPAC Guideline for Disinfection and Sterilization in Healthcare Facilities. https://www.cdc.gov/infectioncontrol/pdf/guidelines/disinfection-guidelines.pdf
- Diligence in Infection Prevention is Key to Maintaining the Quality of Laundered Healthcare Textiles (Sehulster, L). http://www.infectioncontroltoday.com/articles/2017/10/diligence-in-infection-prevention-is-key-to-maintaining-the-quality-of-laundered-healthcare-textiles.aspx
- ECRI Healthcare Hazard Control. Mold Remediation Guidance. https://www.ecri.org/Resources/Hurricane/Mold_Remediation%28Healthcare-Hazard-Control%29.pdf
- Guidelines for Assessment and Remediation of Fungi in Indoor Environments (New York City Department of Health and Mental Hygiene). https://www1.nyc.gov/assets/doh/downloads/pdf/epi/epi-mold-guidelines.pdf
- Healthcare Laundry Accreditation Council Checklist. http://docs.wix-static.com/ugd/076879_a2ad48dc9b1b4f88b826dafd5d4446e6.pdf
- Healthcare Textiles and Laundry 101. https://www.ndhealth.gov/disease/hai/Docs/WebEx/NDHCFLaundry11162011.pdf
- How to Handle Contaminated Linens. Infection Control Today. http://www.infectioncontroltoday.com/articles/2005/08/how-to-handle-contaminated-linens.aspx
- IAHCSMM Central Service Department: A Shared Need. https://www.iahcsmm.org/resource-documents/cs-sample-documents.html
- Infection Prevention for Dummies (Free). http://darrelhicks.com/dummies
- NIOSH Cleaning & Disinfecting Environmental Surfaces in Health Care Facilities. https://ac.els-cdn.com/S0196655315000759/1-s2.0-S0196655315000759-main.pdf?_tid=a12b0b46-d3ac-11e7-830d-00000aacb360&acdnat=1511812585_6580526a5ec82d805f73e97a4e6c9b59

- NIOSH Hydrogen Peroxide References. https://www.cdc.gov/niosh/topics/hydrogen-peroxide/default.html
- NIOSH Pocket Guide for Chemical Hazards: Hydrogen Peroxide. https://www.cdc.gov/niosh/npg/npgd0335.html
- OSHA Hurricane eMatrix: Building Assessment, Restoration, and Demolition Mold Remediation. https://www.osha.gov/SLTC/etools/hurricane/mold.html
- OSHA NIOSH INFOSHEET Protecting Workers Who Use Cleaning Chemicals. https://www.osha.gov/Publications/OSHA3512.pdf
- OSHA Hospital e-TOOL Central Supply. https://www.osha.gov/SLTC/etools/hospital/central/central.html
- WHO Guidelines for Indoor Air Quality: Dampness & Mould. http://www.euro.who.int/__data/assets/pdf_file/0017/43325/E92645.pdf

References

American Industrial Hygiene Association. (1997). *The occupational environment – Its evaluation and control*. AIHA Press. Fairfax, VA, USA.

American Society of Heating, Refrigerating and Air-conditioning Engineers, Inc. (1999, 2013). *Ventilation for indoor air quality. ASHRAE standard 62-1999* (pp. 1–27). Atlanta, GA: ASHRAE.

Burden, M., et al. (2011). Newly cleaned physician uniforms and infrequently washed white coats have similar rates of bacterial contamination after an 8-hour workday: A randomized controlled trial. *Journal of Hospital Medicine., 6*(4), 177–182.

California Occupational Safety and Health Administration. §5199. Aerosol Transmissible Diseases. Subchapter 7. General Industry Safety Orders. Group 16. Control of Hazardous Substances. Article 109. Hazardous Substances and Processes. 2009.

CDC. (2008). *HICPAC guideline for disinfection and sterilization in healthcare facilities*.

CDC. (2008). *Protect yourself and others – use sharps with safety features*. https://www.cdc.gov/sharpssafety/pdf/sharpssafety_poster3.pdf

CDC. (2019). *Molds in the environment*. https://www.cdc.gov/mold/faqs.htm

Fijan, S., & Turk, S. (2012). Hospital textiles, are they a possible vehicle for healthcare-associated infections? *International Journal of Environmental Research and Public Health, 9*, 3330–3343.

HICPAC, CDC. (2008) Guideline for Disinfection and Sterilization in Healthcare Facilities, 2008.

International Safety Center. (2019). *EPINet needlestick and sharp object injury report, 2019*.

Mitchell, A., et al. (2015, Aug). Role of healthcare apparel and other healthcare textiles in the transmission of pathogens: A review of the literature. *The Journal of Hospital Infection, 90*(4), 285–292.

OSHA. 29 CFR 1910.1030. Bloodborne Pathogens Standard. 1991, 2001.

OSHA. (n.d.). *Healthcare wide hazards needlesticks/sharps injuries*. https://www.osha.gov/SLTC/etools/hospital/hazards/sharps/sharps.html#bluntingneedles

Chapter 10
Personal Protective Equipment Placement and Use

> **Objectives**
> - Provide background on the position of PPE in the hierarchy of controls.
> - Identify the role of PPE in health care and barriers to use.
> - Describe standards and specifications for PPE and their application in health care.
> - Provide information on selection of each PPE type.
> - Provide a list of tools and resources.

PPE's Role in the Hierarchy of Controls

There is no doubt that key to preventing occupational exposure to infectious disease in health care is the availability and use of personal protective equipment (PPE). PPE used in health care is designed not only to keep pathogenic microorganisms immediately off clothes, skin, and hair, but also to filter out any that can get into one's eyes, nose, or mouth.

Infection preventionists may elude to the use of PPE for protection of the patient, but this is not what PPE is intended for. It is intended for personal, meaning self-protection, to protect the wearer (the worker) from hazards in their environment.

PPE when effectively selected and appropriately used can be a very effective tool for hazard control. Based on what we know, PPE can be cast across two broad and opposing spectrums.

- One – as it sits at the bottom of the hierarchy of controls. The last resort, the last line of defense, the least effective, when all other controls do not successfully protect the worker from a hazard. More on this in a bit.
- Two – the foundation of the hierarchy of controls. The bedrock, the first line of defense for a worker against a hazard when he or she does not know if the other

© Springer Nature Switzerland AG 2020
A. H. Mitchell, *Preventing Occupational Exposures to Infectious Disease in Health Care*, https://doi.org/10.1007/978-3-030-56039-3_10

controls in the hierarchy are in place and working or not, or if a hazard is completely unknown.

As it relates to the second, however, one essential point for the rights of workers must not be overlooked. The worker should *always* know what controls are in place to protect them from hazards in their work environment. It is the employer's duty to make sure that hazards are adequately assessed and that they are clearly communicated to their workforce. If this is not true, the employees know that they have the ability (and duty) to speak out and to file a complaint without negative consequence, penalty, discrimination, or repercussion.

OSHA standards are in place for employers to protect workers as the Hippocratic oath is in place for physicians to protect patients – first do no harm. This is a worker's right and an employer's legal responsibility.

This may all seem dramatic; after all, PPE is used in nearly all workplaces, every day, sometimes all day. What's the big deal?

The big deal is this: While there are manufacturing standards and specifications for PPE, many are voluntary, and even the best designed PPE can fail. The success in protecting workers from hazards, especially microscopic hazards like pathogens, depends on the ability for the PPE to work like it claims to work. It also depends on the ready availability (accessibility) of PPE immediately when it is needed and the appropriate and effective donning (putting on) and doffing (taking off) by the worker. Finally, PPE is only successful in protecting those in the work environment if it is disposed of safely, so that no one downstream becomes contaminated with whatever was on it. If any of these underlying factors are breached, the links are severed, and the chain of protection is broken.

These are some of the reasons why occupational health experts agree that PPE sits at the bottom (least effective end) of the hierarchy of controls. Employers and their staff should not rely on PPE exclusively for hazard control; it must be used in conjunction with other controls in the hierarchy.

Barriers to PPE Use and Compliance

PPE is not designed to protect the wearer from all pathogenic hazards under all conditions in a healthcare setting. As the world learned from the Ebola crisis in 2014, and is learning during the COVID-19 pandemic, PPE itself can produce additional hazards when worn for long periods of time in hot environments, including heat stress, reduced mobility, dexterity, and tactility, as well as impaired vision, hearing, and ability to carry out safe clinical procedures on patients (Kohn and Ferry 1999).

Healthcare environments are unique for PPE because while it is important to protect the worker from the pathogenic hazard, it is oftentimes more important to protect the patient from undue harm in the form of a medical error. This is one of the underlying reasons why compliance with PPE use is lower than ideal. Healthcare providers do not want to unduly frighten their patient dressed in "full gear," nor do they want to compromise their ability to perform delicate procedures. Other reasons for lack of compliance is discomfort, inability to reconcile protection for worker and/or performing adequate patient care, lack of time, lack of access, forgetfulness, and lack of training (Efstathiou et al. 2011). Related to respiratory protection, it is important to remember that surgical masks are not considered PPE. They are in place to protect the patient from the wearer – physician, nurse, technician, etc. – not the wearer from the patient.

Data from EPINet shows that while nearly 90% of all splashes and splatters of blood and/or body fluids occurred to the head/face (48.1% to eyes), face PPE was only worn 6.9% of the time (mask, eye protection, faceshield) (EPINet 2019). Not one employee indicated wearing a respirator. This is sure to change with 2020 data relative to COVID-19. We already know that mucous membrane exposures to bloodborne and infectious diseases are extremely high risk and that since PPE wear is so low for these types of exposures, a great deal of focus is needed to improve protection for those working in health care. Given the current state of the COVID-19 pandemic, as well as the increasing use of PPE in health care, it is hopeful that these trends will change and improve in years to come. It is unfortunate that it may take a pandemic to improve safety measures that should have been in place all along.

The Importance of PPE's Role in Protection

With all of that being so, PPE does still absolutely have an important place in pre-venting occupational exposures to infectious disease in healthcare settings – *especially* in healthcare settings. PPE, in this case, also works to protect the environment and the patient from the individual worker. With extremely immunocompromised patients, like those in transplant or oncology units, this is important to prevent cross-contamination to them.

PPE use is important for all personnel with potential exposure to pathogenic microorganisms, but especially those at the patient bedside providing direct patient care. Nurses sustain almost half (49.3%) of all reported blood and body fluid exposures (EPINet 2019). However, exposures are frequently reported by all clinical professions, including physicians, clinical laboratory professionals, environmental services, EMS, transporters, technicians and technical trades, and in all settings where care is provided and research is performed including emergency services, home care, and research facilities.

Selection of appropriate PPE based on not only hazard but the type of work environment where the hazard is encountered is essential to creating an effective barrier without creating other secondary hazards associated with its use as described above.

PPE Standards and Specifications

NIOSH posits that "workers are more likely to appropriately use PPE when they are confident that the equipment will provide the intended protections based on its conformance with appropriate standards" (NIOSH 2017). These standards include consensus standards developed by mostly volunteer-expert-run organizations like

ASTM International, AAMI (Association for the Advancement of Medical Instrumentation), and ISO (International Organization of Standardization).

While this may certainly be true, realistically most healthcare workers are focused on patient care standards and not focused on keeping up with the latest manufacturing standards. Therefore, resources like this one can assist those responsible for occupational infection prevention in providing documentation, resources, and tools to include in employee training and to keep on hand for reference.

There are many standards in place that govern PPE use in healthcare facilities including those detailed in Chap. 5, but none are very specific. For example, the OSHA Bloodborne Pathogens Standard states the following:

> When there is occupational exposure, the employer shall provide, at no cost to the employee, appropriate personal protective equipment such as, but not limited to, gloves, gowns, laboratory coats, face shields or masks and eye protection, and mouthpieces, resuscitation bags, pocket masks, or other ventilation devices. (OSHA 1991, 2001)

This language is "performance-based," meaning that it is intentionally broad and leaves methods of compliance with this requirement up to the employer based on their exposure assessment and the circumstances under which the employee deems if:

> …(in their) professional judgment that in the specific instance its use would have prevented the delivery of health care or public safety services or would have posed an increased hazard to the safety of the worker or co-worker.

Standards like this one, because it focuses on one hazard – bloodborne pathogens – is useful, but not prescriptive. Other PPE standards, like OSHA's Personal Protective Equipment Standard (29 CRF 1910.132), is even more broad – even vague – and less prescriptive because it is intended to consider PPE availability, selection, and use in all general industries. This problem was encountered and very publicly visible during the COVID-19 pandemic, where there was so much confusion about what level of PPE is most effective to prevent transmission of a novel virus. It is hopeful that future guidance and regulatory text from national organizations and agencies is more prescriptive and specific.

One of the reasons why a practical resource guide like this may be so useful is to help specify when and what PPE should be selected and used based on the hazard specific to this book – infectious disease.

PPE and Protective Apparel

Being methodical about PPE selection, availability, and use involves careful attention to your facility's Exposure and Hazard Assessments (covered in detail in Chap. 7). It is during those activities that special focus is spent on determining what types of exposures might affect what body part or whether they may potentially expose an entire body to an infectious microorganism.

The National Academies of Sciences, Engineering, and Medicine (the Academies) indicate that "for the consumer or worker, conformity assessment provides confidence in the claims made about the product by the manufacturer and may assist the consumer with purchasing decisions in determining the fitness of a product for it its intended use" (IOM 2017).

For PPE, there are many conformity or consensus standards in place, as well as some mandatory requirements.

Applicable PPE Standards and Recommendations

- OSHA Personal Protective Equipment 29 CFR 1910.132
- OSHA Respiratory Protection Standard 29 CFR 1910.134
- OSHA Bloodborne Pathogens Standard 29 CFR 1910.1030
- California Only: Aerosol Transmissible Diseases Standard §5199
- NIOSH-Approved Particulate Filtering Facepiece Respirators (Surgical N95, N99, P100, PAPR)
- FDA Medical Glove Guidance Manual 21 CFR 880.6250, 21 CFR 878.4460
- FDA Surgical Apparel 21 CFR 878.4040

  - Includes surgical caps, hoods, masks, gowns, operating room shoes and shoe covers, and isolation masks and gowns

OSHA's standards for eye and face protection, head protection, foot protection, and several others specific to PPE type are for physical hazards that do not specifically include bloodborne or infectious disease hazards. OSHA has, however, interpreted that the standards do apply to biological hazards (OSHA 2011).

FDA guidance that is in place for premarket notification (FDA "clearance") focuses on protecting patient and consumers, rather than workers. However, the standards provide useful for understanding how performance is measured and what testing is required to be performed by manufacturers to ensure that PPE does what it claims to do.

PPE performance consensus standards from organizations like ASTM International, AAMI, and ISO are available, but only for purchase or in limited availability with membership. As such, they are not listed here, but you can find a list of links in the Tools and Resources section of this chapter. In general, ASTM guidance assists in the identification and application of the most appropriate standards for the assessment, development of specifications, and selection of medical PPE "with the ultimate goal of maintaining the safety and health of healthcare workers who may come into contact with biological and chemical hazards" (ASTM 2019).

Gloves

Gloves and protective handwear are designed to protect the worker from exposure to pathogenic microorganisms and other contaminants (hazardous drugs, detergents, disinfectants, sterilants, etc.) and must be evaluated and selected based on their material makeup and its ability to the worker from the specific hazard. In health care, gloves perform double duty. They protect worker from patient and environment and patient from worker.

The absolute most important thing to keep in mind about glove use is that appropriate timing of donning (putting on) and doffing (taking off) gloves is critical. If gloves are put on too soon before touching a patient and performing a clinical procedure on them, the gloves themselves can become a vector, as they get potentially contaminated with environmental pathogens from, say, touching the bed rail or infusion pump or countertop or your face. For patients with indwelling catheters and compromised immunity, a transfer of an environmental pathogenic organism could have dire consequences.

Timing for doffing and adequate disposal is equally as important, not so much for the patient, but for the worker themselves as well as anyone that comes into contact with that contaminated glove downstream. Gloves should be immediately removed after touching a potential contaminated source (patient, specimen, body fluid cleanup, etc.) and disposed of in the trash or red bag (depending on whether they are contaminated with blood or body fluids).

Since many people experience allergies to latex and powders, be sure to select gloves that are safe and effective for staff. Since space is limited in patient care settings, it is important to have a variety of glove types available for employees based on your facility's exposure assessment.

Gowns

Like gloves, gowns serve two purposes: first, to protect the wearer from splashes and splatters with blood and body fluids, as well as microbial contamination to their clothes and uniforms; second, for patients on isolation or contact precautions, gowns serve to protect them from whatever contamination is on their care provider's uniform.

It is important to reiterate that scrubs are uniforms. They are not PPE; therefore, they need to be covered by gowns when an exposure is possible. Ideally, healthcare organizations would prohibit scrubs from being worn outside of work and dictate that employees change into street clothes. This serves multiple purposes, protecting outside environment, the public, and the home from contamination.

There are various standards for gown performance, including specifications for types of anticipated exposures – high transmissibility (for pathogens like Ebola), splash/spray velocity (for something like orthopedic surgeries), and fluid repellency. They range from the following criteria established by FDA (FDA 2016):

- Level 1: *Minimal risk* – to be used, for example, during basic care, standard isolation, cover gown for visitors, or in a standard medical unit
- Level 2: *Low risk* – to be used, for example, during blood draw, suturing, in the intensive care unit (ICU), or a pathology lab
- Level 3: *Moderate risk* – to be used, for example, during arterial blood draw, inserting an intravenous (IV) line, in the emergency room, or for trauma cases

- Level 4: *High risk* – to be used, for example, during long, fluid-intense procedures, surgery, when pathogen resistance is needed or infectious diseases are suspected (non-airborne)

There seem to be more standards set for the performance and design features of gowns by standards-setting organizations than for any other type of PPE. Many of these standards are listed in "Tools and Resources" at the end of this chapter.

- US Food and Drug Administration (FDA)
- Association of periOperative Registered Nurses (AORN)
- ASTM International (formerly the American Society for Testing and Materials)
- American National Standards Institute (ANSI)
- Association for the Advancement of Medical Instrumentation (AAMI)
- American Association of Textile Chemists and Colorists (AATCC)

Gown selection should be done in partnership with surgical, infection prevention, materials management/supply chain, and OHS/EHS to be sure that the right gowns are selected for the right performance and that they are placed exactly where they are needed to improve wear compliance. There must also be decisions made about whether a facility uses disposable or reusable (cloth) gowns. If reusable gowns are being used, it is essential to have safe containerization, labeling, and laundering protocols in place. Environmental services (EVS) and laundry personnel need to be aware of potential risks they may face relative to aeration of contaminants as they sort and process linen.

Eye Protection and Faceshields

Since more than 50% of all blood and body fluid exposures are to the unprotected eye (EPINet 2019), this is where a good deal of focus should be. Early adopter healthcare facilities are requiring eye protection to be worn while performing all patient care or clinical laboratory work. They institute eye protection programs similar to those in manufacturing where one must not step foot on the manufacturing floor without donning protective eyewear.

Eye exposures not only are painful but also can result in potential exposure to not just a bloodborne pathogen, but also bacteria, fungi, or spores, to name a few, and, like multidrug-resistant organisms like MRSA, has a high affinity to enter via mucous membranes. Unlike other body fluid splatter exposures, those to the eyes require a caregiver to step away from the patient or task at hand and find an eye wash station and report to employee health. This interrupts the flow of work and can result in some rather traumatic emotional and psychological effects.

Eye exposures, even to respiratory pathogens, happen. This was learned during the COVID-19 pandemic. The process is a bit involved, but simply, the "nasolacrimal duct" connects to tear ducts and drains into the nose. It can drain through the front of the nose or through the back of the nose through the paranasal sinus into the back of the throat and into the trachea, the bronchus, and then the lungs.

Eye exposures should be avoided at all costs, and careful attention needs to be paid to not only providing eye protection but also making it immediately accessible where it's needed. This includes considerations for patient and exam rooms, operating rooms, and ICUs, as typically 70% or more of all eye exposures occur in these areas. Of those, about 40% occur in patient/exam rooms where wall caddies can be installed to save valuable counter space (EPINet 2019).

Important considerations need to be made for eye protection type. Protective eyewear comes in the form of disposable and reusable eyewear, goggles, eyeglasses with side shields, and faceshields. When bending and moving, slippage can occur resulting in potential exposures into the eye around the eyewear. In determining eyewear type, this has to fit into the decision-making criteria as does maintaining clear sight so that medical procedures can be done safely and effectively. Also, for people wearing prescription eyeglasses, fit over glasses needs to be considered, as well as whether prescription eye protection should be purchased by employers. There are so many options available today that fit any and all needs.

Today, with employee onboarding, an essential consideration could be to provide new employees with not only their badge and benefits package but also a choice of the eye protection of their liking. This could include fun and interesting designs and colors, if using reusable eye protection. It could also include a health benefit option of prescription eye protection. For facilities using disposable eye protection, many are hanging caddies in patient and procedure rooms to increase accessibility and cues to action as described in Chap. 8.

Masks and Respirators

First thing is first: surgical/medical masks are not respirators and respirators are not masks. Many occupational health experts will say that masks should not be considered PPE at all because they are intended to protect the patient and do not offer any protection to the healthcare worker wearing it. Masks are intended to protect the patient from the wearer and not the wearer from the patient or microorganisms. Surgical masks are designed to be fluid resistant from large droplets and sprays (mucus) only, and since they are not tightly fitted, air readily flows into and out of the breathing zone. Procedure and isolation masks are not fluid resistant; they are meant to be worn into an isolation room for non-aerosol-generating procedures to protect the patient from exposure to a microorganism that may cause a healthcare-associated infection. More information about masks compared to respirators especially as it relates to OSHA compliance is available in Chap. 5.

During a time of uncertainty, like the COVID-19 pandemic, it can be an important process to have patients that are experiencing symptoms (cough, fever, runny nose, etc.) to have masks available for them to wear upon entry to the building. This serves to protect not only those working in the healthcare facility but also any other people in the building (patients, families, vendors, and more). Using face coverings like cloth masks do prove useful for people going out in public, like to the grocery store or other business.

That said, there are specifications in place for surgical/medical masks including design and testing criteria for bacterial filtration efficiency, differential pressure, submicron particulate filtration efficiency, resistance to penetration by synthetic blood, and flammability. They also offer a physical barrier that can decrease the likelihood that a healthcare worker inadvertently touches their nose, eyes, and mouth and then touches the patient.

According to NIOSH, "(s)urgical masks provide barrier protection against droplets including large respiratory particles. Most surgical masks do not effectively filter small particles from the air and do not prevent leakage around the edge of the mask when the user inhales" (NIOSH 2015). In cases where filtration of small particles like microorganisms is required, a respiratory protection program must be implemented. NIOSH, not FDA, is the leading authority on respirators and serves as the "approval" authority. Table 10.1 offers guidance on appropriate selection of masks and respirators.

Healthcare facilities are required to have respiratory protection programs in place per OSHA standards (29 CFR 1910.134), and we covered some of the requirements under this standard in Chap. 5. During the exposure assessment phase in your facility and when new procedures are being performed or new infectious disease

Table 10.1 Surgical masks, filtering facepiece respirators, and surgical respirators

Surgical masks		Filtering facepiece respirators	Surgical respirators
Intended use when:	Depends on facilities hazard assessment plan. Does not protect against small airborne particles (aerosols)	Reduce healthcare provider (HCP) inhalation of both large droplets and small airborne particles (aerosols)	Reduce HCP inhalation of both large droplets and small airborne particles (aerosols)
Work by healthcare personnel (HCP)	Protect the patient and sterile filed by reducing the number of particles introduced into the room as HCP talk, sneeze, or cough. Protect the wearer's nose/mouth from splashes or sprays of large droplets of body fluid	Protect the patient by reducing the number of particles introduced into the room as HCP talk, sneeze, or cough	Protect the patient and sterile field by reducing the number of particles introduces into the room as HCP talk, sneeze, or cough. Protect the wearer's nose/mouth from splashed or sprays of large droplets of body fluids
Worn by patient	Protect HCP by reducing the number of particles introduced into the room as patients talks, sneezes, or coughs	Not typically worn by patients	Not typically worn by patients
Fit testing required?	No, not designed to seal to the face	Yes, to ensure adequate seal to the face	Yes, to ensure adequate seal to the face
Government oversight	FDA clears for marketing	NIOSH provides certification	NIOSH provides certification and FDA clears for marketing

hazards emerge, this is when the respirator type (particulate filtration; filtering face-piece respirators) should be identified, selected, and made available (N95, N99, P100, PAPR, elastomeric, etc.). This has to include considerations for storage, disposal and/or reprocessing.

Some useful tools are available in the Tools and Resources section including those from OSHA, NIOSH, CDC, and ASTM. The best resource for managing respiratory protection programs in health care is a joint document from OSHA and NIOSH called "Hospital Respiratory Protection Program Toolkit: Resources for Respirator Program Administrators." It provides extremely useful guidance, recommendations, and decision-making paradigms for you to determine, along with infection prevention and control, what is best for your facility based on your patient mix, procedures performed, and geography.

It also aids in the determination of selection of surgical masks versus respirators and sometimes both (mask on patient, respirator on worker), as well as if fit testing and medical evaluation is required. NIOSH defines "surgical respirators" as filtering facepiece respirators with spray- and splash-resistant facemask material on the outside to protect the wearer (NIOSH 2015).

Since respirators often protect against that which we cannot see because they are tightly fitted, implementation of and compliance to the programs can get complicated. This is exactly the reason why there are so many terrific resources available to you for free.

Shoe and Head Covers

Shoe and head covers do serve as a physical barrier when sprays, splatters, and splashes of blood, body fluids, and other potentially infectious materials occur, but they are mostly worn in healthcare settings to protect the patient and to keep "sterile" areas like the operating room free from excess contamination. Organizations like AORN and American College of Surgeons have guidance on these types of PPE. Guidance from professional societies like these are typically only available for purchase, but there are some useful papers and blogs that are available for everyone to read (AORN 2017, ACS 2017).

Head covers like surgical caps are typically "personalized" from practitioner to practitioner and are purchased and brought in. Some facilities have moved away from this model and supply them just as they do scrubs used in the operating room. Whatever the case, be sure that there are processes and procedures in place to address laundering these items from use to use and when/if they are contaminated with blood and body fluids. Shoe covers and bouffant style head covers tend to be single-use disposable items and as such making sure there is enough in stock and a proper location to house them that is immediately accessible when needed.

PPE Selection and Implementation Plan

- Conduct the risk assessment (based on your exposure assessment, Chap. 7).
- Use information from assessment to determine appropriate PPE.
- Choose applicable PPE design, functionality, and performance.
- Establish PPE program, including fit testing (if applicable), training, accessibility/placement, disposal, replacement.
- Evaluate plan, including surveillance data based on exposure incidents and PPE use/wear.

Accessibility and Placement

Driving compliance with PPE can oftentimes depend solely on one thing – access. If PPE is not placed in locations where it is needed, when it is needed, not only will it not be worn, but healthcare workers take on unacceptable risk of exposure to an infectious microorganism. In some cases, workers not only take on this risk, but so do patients and frequently, patient safety is the primary driver for change at a leadership level. Those of us in the worker safety field hate to admit that patient safety drives safety and quality decisions in health care, but since the patient is the "product," it is certainly true.

Many facilities are utilizing wall- or door-mounted PPE caddies, some in the form of "infection control" caddies that house items for contact or isolation precautions (gowns, gloves, masks). Custom caddies (wall mounted and door hangers) can be made that also include eye protection, respirators, and even shoe or head covers. As mentioned earlier, eye exposures are the most prevalent reported incident type, and the majority is happening in the patient/exam room.

You are encouraged to look through the facility's OSHA recordable exposures (those requiring more than just first aid – mucous membrane and non-intact skin incidents) and near miss/hit data (if collected) to identify where exposures are occurring and if, when they are occurring, the staff member is wearing PPE or not. EPINet data can tell you this, and if you do not already use it, it is free to use and easy to download (www.internationalsafetycenter.org/use-epinet).

Facilities with a strong operational culture of safety record "near misses". For example, near misses can include medication doses that are recognized as incorrect prior to administration or failure to clearly mark the right site for a surgery. Recording these almost catastrophic incidents create increased visibility to errors that could have happened so that they can be prevented in the future. They can serve as a basis for creating occupational checklists, similar to surgical checklists.

An example of an occupational exposure near miss could be failure to have ready access to eye protection when a face exposure occurs, despite it not actually getting into the eyes, or a splash to a lab coat or scrubs that results in the worker having to change their uniform when PPE is not being worn.

Doing some data mining will help in identifying if PPE is placed where it is needed. Simple rounds will help with this as well, so that you can physically see where PPE is placed and if the appropriate PPE is placed based on the exposure assessment.

PPE carts can be a good idea, but then it relies on the carts being accessible to all staff on unit when and where it is needed. Sometimes this is an instantaneous need in the event of an emergent code and time cannot be taken to locate the cart in order to provide timely and urgent care to the patient. This is one reason why placement inside every patient, procedure, and exam room is a more effective model.

As a final thought, to loop back to where we started in this chapter, PPE may be at the bottom of the hierarchy of controls. It may be used when all other controls do not afford the worker the best protection possible, but it is a critical element to any great occupational infection prevention and control program. It protects both personnel and patients from hazards that we cannot see and may not anticipate. Because many exposures in health care are not able to be foreseen, we must learn from our exposure surveillance data and let it light our path so that future exposures can be prevented.

Since so many facilities are struggling with the best ways to protect their workforce as it relates to PPE, many facilities around the world are considering the adoption of engineered, protective textiles for uniforms, lab coats, and scrub jackets that include the design of materials that are fluid repellent and/or antimicrobial (Mitchell et al. 2015). There are several on the market, and more and more are available every year. These types of "technical textiles" may need to be evaluated and selected at your facility as a way to add a layer of protection where one had not previously existed. Think of these types of textile advancements as protective uniforms that are worn throughout the work shift and provide an engineering control for what you wear.

Tools and Resources
- AAMI Levels and Surgical Gowns: Know if You're Protected (Pfiedler Enterprises). http://www.pfiedler.com/ce/1191/files/assets/common/downloads/AAMI%20levels%20and%20surgical%20gowns;%20know%20if%20you.pdf
- ASTM D7103–06(2013) Standard Guide for Assessment of Medical Gloves. https://www.astm.org/Standards/D7103.htm
- ASTM D6319–10(2015) Standard Specification for Nitrile Examination Gloves for Medical Application. https://www.astm.org/Standards/D6319.htm
- ASTM D5250–06(2015) Standard Specification for Poly(vinyl chloride) Gloves for Medical Application. https://www.astm.org/Standards/D5250.htm
- ASTM D6977–04(2016) Standard Specification for Polychloroprene Examination Gloves for Medical Application. https://www.astm.org/Standards/D6977.htm

- ASTM D6978–05(2013) Standard Practice for Assessment of Resistance of Medical Gloves to Permeation by Chemotherapy Drugs. https://www.astm.org/Standards/D6978.htm
- ASTM F1862/F1862M – 17 Standard Test Method for Resistance of Medical Face Masks to Penetration by Synthetic Blood (Horizontal Projection of Fixed Volume at a Known Velocity). https://www.astm.org/Standards/F1862.htm
- ASTM F2100–11 Standard Specification for Performance of Materials Used in Medical Face Masks. https://www.astm.org/Standards/F2100.htm
- ASTM F2407–06(2013)e1 Standard Specification for Surgical Gowns Intended for Use in Healthcare Facilities. https://www.astm.org/Standards/F2407.htm
- (Note: All ASTM Standards not listed here can be found on their website at www.astm.org. Unfortunately, ASTM Standards are available for purchase only.)
- CDC Protecting Healthcare Personnel. https://www.cdc.gov/hai/prevent/ppe.html
- CDC Sequence for Removing Personal Protective Equipment (PPE) (English & Spanish). https://www.cdc.gov/HAI/pdfs/ppe/ppeposter148.pdf
- CDC PPE in Healthcare Facilities, Trainer's Information. https://www.cdc.gov/hai/prevent/ppe_train.html
- FDA Masks and N95 Respirators. https://www.fda.gov/MedicalDevices/ProductsandMedicalProcedures/GeneralHospitalDevicesandSupplies/PersonalProtectiveEquipment/ucm055977.htm
- FDA Medical Glove Guidance Manual. https://www.fda.gov/downloads/MedicalDevices/DeviceRegulationandGuidance/GuidanceDocuments/UCM428191.pdf
- FDA Medical Gowns. https://www.fda.gov/MedicalDevices/Products and-MedicalProcedures/GeneralHospitalDevicesandSupplies/PersonalProtectiveEquipment/ucm452775.htm
- FDA Premarket Notification Requirements Concerning Gowns Intended for Use in Health Care Settings. https://www.fda.gov/downloads/MedicalDevices/DeviceRegulationandGuidance/GuidanceDocuments/UCM452804.pdf
- FDA "Personal Protective Equipment Regulated by FDA" Training Powerpoint (S Murphey). http://www.nationalacademies.org/hmd/~/media/BE4C13B1BC4143CBB6B40BA38D13792C.ashx
- NIOSH Filtering out Confusion: Frequently Asked Questions about Respiratory Protection. https://www.cdc.gov/niosh/npptl/FilteringOutConfusion.html
- NIOSH Healthcare Respiratory Protection Resources. https://www.cdc.gov/niosh/npptl/hospresptoolkit/default.html
- NIOSH/OSHA Hospital Respiratory Protection Program Toolkit. https://www.cdc.gov/niosh/docs/2015-117/pdfs/2015-117.pdf

- NIOSH National Framework for Personal Protective Equipment Conformity Assessment – Infrastructure. https://www.cdc.gov/niosh/docs/2018-102/pdfs/2018-102.pdf
- NIOSH-Approved Powered Air-Purified Respirators Meeting CDC Criteria for Ebola. https://www.cdc.gov/niosh/npptl/topics/respirators/disp_part/paprtables.html
- NIOSH-Approved N95 Particulate Filtering Facepiece Respirators. https://www.cdc.gov/niosh/npptl/topics/respirators/disp_part/n95list1.html
- NIOSH-Approved Particulate Filtering Facepiece Respirators. https://www.cdc.gov/niosh/npptl/topics/respirators/disp_part/default.html
- NIOSH PPE Case Testing of Stockpiled ANSI/AAMI PB70 Level 4 Surgical Gowns. https://www.cdc.gov/niosh/npptl/pdfs/FINAL-PPE-CASE-7-17-17.pdf
- NIOSH Protective Clothing and Ensembles Resource. https://www.cdc.gov/niosh/npptl/pce.html
- NIOSH Respirator Trusted Source Information. https://www.cdc.gov/niosh/npptl/topics/respirators/disp_part/RespSource3healthcare.html
- OSHA Respiratory Protection Program Plan. https://www.osha.gov/sites/default/files/2019-03/respiratoryprotection.pdf
- OSHA Respiratory Protection Training Videos. https://www.osha.gov/SLTC/respiratoryprotection/training_videos.html
- OSHA Respirator Medical Evaluation Questionnaire. https://www.osha.gov/Publications/OSHA3789info.pdf
- Putting On and Removing Personal Protective Equipment (NEJM Videos in Clinical Medicine). http://www.nejm.org/doi/full/10.1056/NEJMvcm1412105?rss=searchAndBrowse&
- Quizlet Hospital PPE Video- Infection Control: Donning and Doffing. https://quizlet.com/162201811/hospital-ppe-video-infection-control-donning-and-doffing-flash-cards/

Acknowledgments Chapter 10, Table 10.1, and Appendix B (Model Exposure Control Plan) were drafted with leadership from Cadence Lutz. Thank you for being beside me on this journey.

References

Association of peri-Operative Registered Nurses. (2017, October). Surgical head coverings: A literature review. *AORN J, 106*(4), 306–316. http://shop.aorn.org/surgical-head-coverings-a-literature-review/.
ASTM D7103 – 06. (2013). *Standard guide for assessment of medical gloves*. https://www.astm.org/Standards/D7103.htm
ASTM F2100 – 11 Standard Specification for Performance of Materials Used in Medical Face Masks. (n.d.). https://www.astm.org/Standards/F2100.htm

ASTM. (2019). Standard Guide for Assessment of Medical Gloves.

Efstathiou, G., et al. (2011). Factors influencing nurses' compliance with standard precautions in order to avoid occupational exposure to microorganisms: A focus group study. *BMC Nursing, 10*, 1. https://bmcnurs.biomedcentral.com/articles/10.1186/1472-6955-10-1.

FDA. (2016). Medical Gowns.

International Safety Center. (2019). EPINet report for blood and body fluid exposure, 2019.

IOM. (2017). National Framework for Personal Protective Equipment Conformity Assessment – Infrastructure.

Kohn, J. P., & Ferry, T. S. (1999). Safety and Health Management. Chapter 21. In J. O. Stull (Ed.), *Personal protective equipment*. Government Issues.

Mitchell, A., et al. (2015). Role of healthcare apparel and other healthcare textiles in the transmission of pathogens: A review of the literature. *J Hosp Infect, 90*(4), 285–292.

NIOSH. (2015). *Hospital respiratory protection program toolkit*. https://www.cdc.gov/niosh/docs/2015-117/pdfs/2015-117.pdf?id=10.26616/NIOSHPUB2015117

NIOSH. (2017). *National framework for personal protective equipment conformity assessment – Infrastructure*. https://www.cdc.gov/niosh/docs/2018-102/default.html

OSHA Bloodborne Pathogens Standard, 29 CFR 1910.1030. (1991, 2001).

OSHA Small Entity Compliance Guide for Respiratory Protection Standard (OSHA 3384-09). (2011).

Chapter 11
Facing a Modern Pandemic

Objectives
- Discuss origin of SARS-CoV-2 and its progression into a pandemic.
- Identify ways to mitigate occupational exposure to SARS-CoV-2 and COVID-19.
- Provide guidance for preventive controls based on lessons learned.

Pandemics are often unpredictable, and their devastating health, economic, and social impacts necessitate continued research to help identify emerging outbreaks. Risk mitigation through careful preparation and planning can abate the subsequent burdens of these devastating events. Since pandemics are those epidemics that cross international borders, they engage governments, organizations, and individuals, requiring multilevel interventions that engage global and local occupational health and safety and infection prevention communities.

The Centers for Disease Control and Prevention (CDC) is instrumental in providing information on the case definition of a new pandemic disease. This includes information on the outbreak source, pathogen identification, modes of transmission, susceptible populations, and guidance on transmission prevention strategies. Other stakeholders include the World Health Organization (WHO), the National Institute for Occupational Safety and Health (NIOSH), the Occupational Safety and Health Administration (OSHA), the National Institute for Environmental Health Sciences (NIEHS), the National Institutes for Health (NIH), and the American Public Health Association (APHA). These organizations often have one common message; however, recommendations may differ primarily if the source pathogen is a new and emerging one, or if the focus is on protecting populations (public health) or workplaces (occupational health). These organizations collaborate with labor organizations, unions, other professional societies, advocacy groups, and community activists to make the greatest impact.

© Springer Nature Switzerland AG 2020
A. H. Mitchell, *Preventing Occupational Exposures to Infectious Disease in Health Care*, https://doi.org/10.1007/978-3-030-56039-3_11

Like an epidemic, a pandemic is an outbreak that impacts a wide geographical area; however, the latter affects countries on multiple continents. In recent years, there have been global efforts to encourage source countries to promptly identify and report outbreaks in order to trigger coordinated, global disaster preparedness efforts against pandemics. Despite these CDC- and WHO-initiated efforts, there continues to be a lag in identifying outbreaks, which ultimately forces affected countries to devise their own prevention efforts.

Global Impact

NIH identifies low- and middle-income countries (LMICs) as those that are most impacted by increased morbidity and mortality associated with pandemics. Pandemics are known to have adverse short- and long-term economic impacts and a decline in global, domestic, and individual activities, such as travel, work, and recreation.

Modern-day outbreaks that have garnered international attention, many of which are discussed in Chap. 2, include the AIDS pandemic in the 1980s; the SARS pandemic of 2003; the H1N1 pandemic, 2009–2010; the West African Ebola epidemic, 2014; the Zika virus epidemic in 2015; and the current COVID-19 pandemic. Pandemic preparedness is particularly challenging because there are myriads of pathogens that have the potential to cause widespread devastation, as demonstrated in the aforementioned events.

When preparing for pandemics, countries should place emphasis on strengthening core public health infrastructure. Strategies for an active pandemic require:

- Continued efforts to improve essential public health support
- Increased public knowledge
- Transmission prevention
- Health care for those infected

The potential for transmission is ongoing, and, as a result, surge capacity based on the magnitude of the potential health burdens must be evaluated. This *Practical Guide* provides tools for facilities to do that.

Determinants of Large-Scale Transmission

A pathogen's potential for large-scale transmission is dependent on its ability to adapt and, probably more importantly, its mode of transmission. This is covered in Chap. 4. The spread of an outbreak is also influenced by certain characteristics of the population, such as density and its risk for infection, transportation and trade patterns, as well as the efficacy of the "public health surveillance and response measures" (Sands et al. 2016). Disease transmission is increased in more dense populations, such as most urban areas like New York City. Other factors that often increase transmission are social inequities, like income inequality and inequality in access to health care, as well as comorbidities, such as diabetes and heart disease.

As mentioned in Chaps. 2, 3, and 4, a key element of infection prevention is to determine the pathogen's modes of transmission. The mode of transmission determines specific control measures that will be used to curtail person-to-person transmission. Many public and private agencies adopt NIOSH's *hierarchy of controls* strategy when they develop occupational infection prevention and control procedures. The measures and controls are detailed in Chap. 3.

Origination of the COVID-19 Pandemic

The cause of the novel coronavirus outbreak remains obscure, but it is widely known that it originated in Wuhan in China's central Hubei province. Chinese officials confirmed the outbreak on December 31, 2019, although it is unclear when the initial infections occurred. It was only a week later that the disease-causing pathogen was identified. The outbreak received more attention when the first patient, a 61-year-old man in Wuhan, succumbed to the illness.

Chinese officials named the local Huanan seafood market as the location where the first cases originated. Many news and social media platforms shared images of wild animals (known reservoirs of coronaviruses) that were believed to be sold illegally at the market.

Western countries tried to determine if the novel virus posed a threat to that side of the hemisphere as the WHO reported that several individuals became infected in Thailand, Japan, and Korea on January 20, 2020.

Just 1 day later, the public learned of the first coronavirus case in the United States. Officials in China implemented quarantine orders in Wuhan (a population of 11 million) on January 23, when all commuting into and out of the city was immediately prohibited. On January 30, WHO confirmed that the outbreak was a public health emergency of international concern with upward of 9000 cases in 19 countries.

The Chinese doctor, Li Wenliang, who was credited for bringing public attention to the virus prior to China's official statement, died from the disease on February 7 in Wuhan. The next 2 days were no less significant: the first US citizen died in Wuhan on February 8, and the next day, a total mortality count of 811 exceeded that of the 2003 SARS epidemic in China. On February 11, WHO made an announcement that the novel coronavirus was responsible for a disease officially called COVID-19. Multiple countries, including Iran and South Korea, reported cases and subsequent deaths over the next few weeks. Those countries, along with Italy, would later be dubbed "hot spots" with notable travel restrictions and advisories. The economic ramifications became more apparent in the United States when the Dow Jones Industrial Average, on February 24, had its biggest decline in 2 years.

COVID-19 Impact on Business, Schools, and Workplaces

Although California announced the first case of COVID-19 in the United States on February 26, it was the state of Washington that reported the first death in the country just 3 days later. The increase in the number of cases fueled efforts to deter large gatherings.

As the world tried to discourage mass gatherings in early March, some countries continued to lose their battle against the pandemic. Countries like Italy responded to its increase in morbidity and mortality with a mass quarantine effort, declaring a lockdown in the northern Lombardy area. The measures proved insufficient at that time as the death toll continued to increase. On March 13, the WHO acknowledged Europe as the "epicenter" of the pandemic, with reports of more cases and deaths in Europe than the rest of the world combined.

The US President declared a national state of emergency on March 13, 2 days after WHO declared a pandemic on March 11, as multiple states, including Michigan, Maryland, and Pennsylvania, expressed plans to close schools. While death tolls increased, it was clear that more needed to be done to prevent the spread of the virus. By mid-March, schools were closing.

Occupational Infection Prevention Guidance

On March 15, the CDC shared their *Interim Guidance for Coronavirus Disease 2019 (COVID-19),* and many private and public organizations used it to implement new policies in order to keep their doors open while protecting their staff (CDC 2020a). Among other recommendations, "social distancing" became one of the main tools used for transmission prevention. Social distancing (physical or spatial distancing) had a tremendous impact on the workforce as "nonessential" workers were told to work from home, and those who lacked the ability to work remotely were furloughed, many without pay. Others lost their jobs. Businesses that remained open operated under the confines of social distancing.

At the time of writing this book, there is no treatment or vaccine for COVID-19. Efforts to curtail transmission of coronavirus involve collaboration among individuals, businesses, local public health authorities, and healthcare institutions. This included quickly identifying a person under investigation (PUI) as someone who has traveled, has symptoms, or has been living with or caring for someone in their household who is sick. Additionally, first responders, law enforcement, and essential workers, such as sanitation and utility workers, are at higher risk because of their interaction with the public.

Many organizations provide guidance for safer operation and day-to-day management of a variety of different types of businesses and industries. These include the CDC, AIHA, NIEHS, labor unions, professional associations, and others. Since this *Practical Guide* focuses on occupational infection prevention in health care, guidance for those other occupations are not mentioned in detail.

Based on a combination of guidance from both public health and occupational health agencies and organizations (CDC 2020a; MDH 2020; OSHA 2020), initial procedures and recommendations for preventing occupational transmission include the following:

- Limit staff exposure to patients and specimens known or suspected to have SARS-CoV-2 infection and/or COVID-19 disease:
  - Have dedicated COVID-19 teams to provide care.
  - Only clinicians and cleaning staff on a limited schedule may enter the patient or procedure room.
  - Critical consultations must be made by specific disciplines only, for example, pulmonology or infectious disease.
- COVID-19 rooms must have correct isolation signs (with PPE information) posted on the doors.
- Respirators, eye protection (goggles/face shield), gown, and gloves need to be worn when caring for patients with known or suspected COVID-19 disease.
- Have a clear channel for staff to access and acquire PPE.
- Record and provide post-exposure follow-up for occupational exposures.
- Have exposed personnel self-isolate for 14 days, as deemed appropriate by occupational health practitioners.
- Symptomatic workers or those confirmed to have COVID-19 must self-isolate for 14 days.
- Have return-to-work clearance in place with ongoing assessment.
- Use EPA-registered products for cleaning, disinfection, and/or sterilization of surfaces (e.g., patient-care items, surfaces).
- Follow instructions for use (IFUs) of products to ensure they are compatible with the type of surfaces and surface material they are used on; this includes contact time.

For common areas like waiting rooms (Fig. 11.1), guidance includes:

- Separate doors for entry and exit if possible
- Dedicated area with hand sanitizer and masks
- Patients required to wear a mask or face covering upon entry
- Limited visitation from friends and family
- Physical distancing of patients in waiting room areas
- Physical barriers (like sneeze guards) to protect personnel

A list of guidance documents is available in the Tools and Resources section of this chapter.

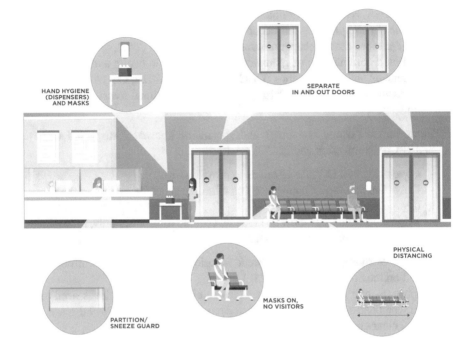

Fig. 11.1 Sample waiting room, triage area. (Source: Chelsey Armstrong (Artist) 2020)

Lessons Learned and Considerations for Ongoing or Future Pandemics

As the number of new COVID-19 cases will ebb and flow and assuredly fade into the background, it is always critical to prepare for after-waves and future outbreaks that can have potential to become epidemics and pandemics. To prepare, we must first assess the protocols, policies, and procedures that we established and relied on for previous disease outbreaks. Were they sufficient? Did they work? If we weren't prepared, why? If we were prepared, how? If we wish we had more time, when? If a single geography or neighborhood fared better or worse, where and why?

Establishing what, why, when, and how healthcare settings identify, establish, and maintain preparation over time have to be grounded firmly in preventing illness and infection in populations of patients, healthcare personnel, and the communities they serve. SARS-CoV-2 held the world at a disadvantage because it was a "novel" virus. But really, was it? If we had prepared healthcare organizations with critical supplies including a variety of respirators, dedicated response teams, adequate patient triage, adequate policies on sick and family leave, robust staffing protocols, and the flexibility to learn along the way, does how a virus react in a human body – as a novelty or not – matter?

In the case of COVID-19, the world found that there were many disadvantages in fighting the pandemic in which limited scientific knowledge about this specific pathogen, coupled with universal lack of PPE, community-based precautions, national consensus, quick action, as well as political disagreements, led to the perfect storm...a storm that leads to a great, reflective calm.

Here is what we learned:

1. We did not remain prepared after ramping up PPE, training, and readiness during the Ebola crisis.
2. Our reliance on vaccines for seasonal outbreaks, like flu, led us to become complacent about preventing other health care and occupationally associated illnesses.
3. Facilities relied on groups of administrators who were removed from clinical practice and followed guidelines set by the CDC with little tailoring to the needs and limitations of the institution.
4. With limited scientific knowledge, it is imperative that transmission-based prevention practices are developed and maintained by a team including occupational health and safety and infection prevention and that an abundance of caution is taken.
5. The availability of PPE was heavily focused on rationing instead of using preventive measures – the rest of the hierarchy of controls – to guide extended use of supplies.
6. Facilities must not have shortages of reliable PPE. When they did and personnel are instructed to reuse PPE, the institution must be willing to support this with parameters for extended use that will keep employees safe.
7. Clear guidance needs to be in place for fatal shortages of PPE with clear pathways for containerizing, cleaning, disinfecting, and redistributing reprocessed PPE like respirators.
8. Frontline users of PPE need to be consulted in order to build the best and safest programs and protocols if there is a limited supply of PPE.
9. If employees believe that the institution has prioritized rationing over their safety, it can destroy the climate and culture of safety and result in unsafe fears, practices, and panic.
10. A priority must be made on competence for surface cleaning and disinfection for all responsible personnel. This is not only the heart of infection prevention but also of overall facility safety and security.
11. For personnel who may be required to wear respirators as part of their job duties, they must be fit-tested as a means of preparation and not panic. Facilities must choose the respirator types they will roll out for each exposure type and fit test as part of updating their exposure control plans, safety data sheets, recordkeeping requirements, and more.
12. Improper respirator fit or doing no fit testing at all contributed to occupational exposures during the outbreak.

13. Diagnostic testing needs to be a part of a facility's preparedness program. This is important for both patients and personnel so that as much knowledge is gained, as soon as possible.
14. Local health departments are woefully underfunded and under-resourced yet serve as one of the richest scientific foundations of occupational health and infection prevention.
15. Contact tracing and employee screening should not be done by nonclinical/non-health-based personnel, as there are strict considerations for maintaining the confidentiality of employee exposure and medical records separate from that of other human resources/employment records. This should be a partnership between the employer and their local department of health/public health.

Additional Considerations

During a pandemic, practitioners of occupational infection prevention also can focus on creating protocols, policies, and procedures around social and physical distancing while employees are at home and out in the community. If healthcare personnel can work remotely, occupational infection preventionists can be important members of the decision-making teams.

Since healthcare personnel have potential exposure not just to patients but also to visitors and vendors, only carefully vetted visitors should be allowed on the units until they are deemed safe to others in order to enter facilities. Additionally, there needs to be increased staff education to communicate a standardized process for every person that enters a facility during an outbreak, epidemic, or pandemic.

Healthcare facilities should consider physical barriers, including "sneeze guards," partitions, barrier controls, and other engineering controls, to prevent the spread of aerosols to staff. Creating physical barriers are good considerations for emergency departments, unit/department check-in, billing, benefits, and in clinical areas, in addition to administrative areas, cafeterias, and cafes.

Since occupational health and safety impacts all working people, a solid emphasis on community-based education and outreach is also key. There are wide chasms of health literacy in many populations. There is misinformation on social media and in the press. Social media has had a major effect on the message that the public receives. Information can contradict scientific findings and fuel fear and, in some cases, neglect. Institutions must take the time to educate the communities they serve and to inform them as much as possible about the outbreak-causing pathogen and what they can do to prevent transmission and keep themselves out of harm's way – both in the community and at work. Ultimately, this reduces the patient burden on healthcare systems when they need full capacity the most.

Tools and Resources
- AIHA Back to Work Safely. https://www.backtoworksafely.org/
- APHA COVID-19. https://apha.org/topics-and-issues/communicable-disease/coronavirus
- CDC Criteria for Return to Work for Healthcare Personnel with Suspected or Confirmed COVID-19. https://www.cdc.gov/coronavirus/2019-ncov/hcp/return-to-work.html
- CDC Information for Healthcare Professionals about Coronavirus (COVID-19). https://www.cdc.gov/coronavirus/2019-ncov/hcp/index.html
- CDC Preparedness Tools for Healthcare Professionals and Facilities Responding to Coronavirus (COVID-19). https://www.cdc.gov/coronavirus/2019-ncov/hcp/preparedness-checklists.html
- CDC PPE Burn Rate Calculator. https://www.cdc.gov/coronavirus/2019-ncov/hcp/ppe-strategy/burn-calculator.html
- CDC Strategies for Optimizing the Supply of N95 Respirators. https://www.cdc.gov/coronavirus/2019-ncov/hcp/respirators-strategy/index.html?CDC_AA_refVal=https%3A%2F%2Fwww.cdc.gov%2Fcoronavirus%2F2019-ncov%2Fhcp%2Frespirator-supply-strategies.html
- ECRI COVID-19 Resources for Clinical Care. https://www.ecri.org/covid-19-resources-clinical-care/
- NIEHS Worker Training Program for COVID-19. https://tools.niehs.nih.gov/wetp/covid19worker/index.cfm
- NIOSH Hospital Respiratory Protection Program Toolkit. https://www.cdc.gov/niosh/docs/2015-117/default.html
- OSHA Healthcare Workers and Employers. https://www.osha.gov/SLTC/covid-19/healthcare-workers.html
- UTHealth COVID-19 Resources (nearly all academic institutions have pages like this). https://www.uth.edu/news/covid-19/
- WHO Guidance for health workers. https://www.who.int/emergencies/diseases/novel-coronavirus-2019/technical-guidance/health-workers

Acknowledgments Forever grateful for the tremendously important contribution to this chapter from Infection Preventionist Denise T. Thompson, MPH, DrPHc, CIC. Her work was the basis for this chapter, for which she was generous enough to contribute amidst caring for patients and fellow colleagues during the height of the COVID-19 pandemic.

Thank you to Paul Landsbergis, PhD, MPH, Department of Environmental and Occupational Health Sciences, School of Public Health, State University of New York (SUNY) Downstate Health Sciences University. Your mentorship, guidance, and review have been so appreciated during the writing of this chapter and throughout my career.

References

CDC. (2020a). *Interim U.S. guidance for risk assessment and work restrictions for healthcare personnel with potential exposure to COVID-19.* https://www.cdc.gov/coronavirus/2019-ncov/hcp/guidance-risk-assesment-hcp.html

Minnesota Department of Health. (2020). *COVID-19 recommendations for health care workers.* https://www.health.state.mn.us/diseases/coronavirus/hcp/hcwrecs.pdf

OSHA. (2020). *Guidance on preparing workplaces for COVID-19.* https://www.osha.gov/Publications/OSHA3990.pdf

Sands, P., El Turabi, A., Saynisch, P. A., & Dzau, V. J. (2016). Assessment of economic vulnerability to infectious disease crises. *Lancet, 388*(10058), 2443–2448. https://doi.org/10.1016/S0140-6736(16)30594-3.

Chapter 12
Making It All Work

Objectives
- Encourage readers to embrace their value as a beacon of public health.
- Provide additional tools and resources for program development and management.
- Summarize key messages described throughout the book.

Champions of Public Health

A pivotal part of making it all work is knowing and owning the following:

> You are a Captain of Public Health! You are the Champion of Safety. You are the Beacon of Wellness. You are the Defender of the Realm. You are Master of Your Universe.

Keeping your workforce safe from microorganisms that may cause illness or infection in your facility means that you have a direct tie to the wellness of your community and ultimately to the public's health.

This is not an overstatement. It is truer than most other roles in health care. Surgeons hold lives in their hands every day. Nurses provide hands-on care to any patient that crosses the threshold of your facility. Clinical laboratorians lead efforts to diagnose disease. Environmental services (EVS) leaders keep the environment safe. Sterile processing personnel keep devices and patient care items safe. Administrative staff keep the organization running smoothly.

You keep them all safe, so they can do their jobs and keep patients safe. After all, remember, without healthcare workers, there is no health care.

If you are responsible for occupational infection prevention and control as an employee or occupational health practitioner or as an infection preventionist or as

© Springer Nature Switzerland AG 2020

A. H. Mitchell, *Preventing Occupational Exposures to Infectious Disease in Health Care*, https://doi.org/10.1007/978-3-030-56039-3_12

an environmental health and safety manager or as risk manager or as a trainer, professor, or teacher, or as a Jack or Jill of all trades, you are powerful.

You are a leader in your organization because they rely on you to help them to provide a working environment that is not only free from recognized harm but that is a place of hope and solace to the community. A place that has the ability to recruit and retain the best workforce. A place that has the ability to actively compete against other similar facilities in your geographic region. A place where people want to work and where patients want to come.

Throughout the pages of this *Practical Guide*, you have been given the background, tools, and resources you need to not only do your job but to do it thoughtfully and well. If there are sections that resonate well with you, copy them and give them out. The chapters are designed to be succinct so that you may share them with others. The book is meant to be carried with you as you need it so that you can mobilize into action when you need to. It can even be a resource that you gift to your colleagues and public health champion friends.

As I write this this very chapter, it is holiday time. My family happens to celebrate Christmas, and the tree is twinkling behind me with the slightest scent of pine, and a choir is angelically singing Christmas songs on my radio. During this time of celebration, rejoicing, and jubilation, I am reflecting not only on this book but on you and the gifts that you bring to society. I am grateful for you and so are so many others. Thank you for the work that you do. Thank you for the selflessness with which you do it.

You may not get smothered with mountains of thanks and gratitude from your co-workers and their patients every day, but I am. There's an army of others like you that are, too. No matter how many days you feel like the police, patrol, or hall monitor, you are not alone.

Onward!

Summary: Requirements and Recommendations

In Chaps. 5 and 6, there are lists and summaries of national requirements, regulations, and guidance. These can serve as the foundation for what you need to focus on, in what areas/locations, and for what employees. They include:

- Bloodborne Pathogens Standard (29 CFR 1910.1030)
- Personal Protective Equipment (29 CFR 1910.132)
- Eye and Face Protection (29 CFR 1910.133)
- Respiratory Protection Standard (29 CFR 1910.134)
- Hazard Communication (29 CFR 1910.1200)
- Recording and Reporting Occupational Injuries and Illnesses (29 CFR 1904)
- General Duty Clause (OSH Act, 5(a)1)
- Cal/OSHA Aerosol Transmissible Disease Standard (for those in California only)
- DOT and EPA labeling and containerization for biomedical materials, diagnostic samples, and hazardous waste

- Viral Hepatitis – Prevention in Health Care
- Information for Healthcare Personnel Potentially Exposed to Hepatitis C Virus (HCV) – Recommended Testing and Follow-up
- Post-exposure prophylaxis, Hepatitis B
- Post-exposure prophylaxis (HIV and other bloodborne pathogens)
- Immunization of Health-Care Personnel: Recommendations of the Advisory Committee on Immunization Practices (ACIP)
- Joint Commission Standards, Environment of Care and Infection Control

Each provides you with a hazard-specific roadmap to follow, so that you can then perform exposure determinations and job hazard assessments as outlined in Chap. 7. These include identifying the following:

- A list of all job classifications in which *all* employees in those job classifications have occupational exposure
- A list of job classifications in which *some* employees have occupational exposure
- A list of all tasks and procedures or groups of closely related task and procedures in which occupational exposure occurs and that are performed by employees (including those "all" and "some")

To help guide your work, it may be helpful to put the results of those ongoing assessments into a table format or "Rounding Checklist" (Table 12.1), which can be updated and edited over time to best reflect what is currently going on in your facility.

When the plan is in place and controls are instituted for each job classification and each procedure/task resulting in potential occupational exposure to infectious disease, and when the training and education is designed, determining the appropriate institutional controls are in place is key to success. Suggestions for increasing visibility to occupational health programs can include elements that improve cues to safe action:

- Visible, well-positioned messages, posters, and/or campaigns
- Ongoing individual feedback, from managers, peers, and patients
- Accessibility of PPE
- Confidence in safer medical device, PPE use, standard precautions, etc.
- Incentives, including financial, physical, emotional, and peer-to-peer

Table 12.1 Rounding checklist

Occupational infection prevention and control rounding checklist							
Strong (S) Moderate (M) Weak (W)	Department/ unit	Responsible person	Engineering control (e.g., safer medical device) use	PPE placement/ use	Infectious/ medical/ sharps waste program	Training and education	Changes needing revision? (e.g., new procedure, phased-out process)

Building Cost-Benefit Models

To leverage current programs or build new ones, it will be necessary to build a financial plan to justify focus and expenditures to leadership. This will include identifying what the financial costs may be of not having a plan in place (reference *Measuring Magnitudes of Severity of Consequences* in Chap. 8).

Consider what the cost, loss, or liability is of the following if an illness or infection were to occur:

- Fatality or permanent health effect
- Severe health effect
- Lost workdays, lost time
- Medical treatment, post-exposure follow-up (prophylaxis)
- Potential lawsuit if exposure results in patient exposure as well

A cost model for each exposure type – think detailed budget – can be an important tool. Table 12.2 shows a sample cost model.

Pulling together this type of cost spreadsheet will entail working closely with materials management, supply chain, and/or central sterile departments. It will be difficult at first, but in the end, it will be worth being able to show facility leadership exactly how much the program costs in comparison to how much is being saved should an exposure happen.

Granted, compliance with national and state regulations and standards is not optional, and outlay of cost needs to happen anyway. But, very few other departments in healthcare institutions know what it costs to keep them going. What "revenue" is generated from providing patient care, dollars from insurance, Medicare, Medicaid, self-pay, reimbursement, etc. can be easier to measure, but for programs like occupational health and safety, this is not the case and should be. Occupational health and safety and infection prevention should not be seen as "cost centers," rather also as potential revenue generators.

Table 12.2 Occupational infection prevention cost model

Exposure	Controls	Responsible department/cost center	Cost
Sharps injuries	Safer medical devices, sharps containers	By department (patient room/unit, OR, ED, PACU, etc.) Materials management Supply chain	
Eye exposures	Eye protection, including goggles, eyewear, faceshields, shrouds	By department (patient room/unit, OR, ED, PACU, etc.) Materials management Supply chain	
Airborne	Respiratory protection program including respirators, fit testing	Employee health	
Contact precautions	Gowns, gloves, hand hygiene products	Infection prevention, infectious disease	

Another important "cost" to measure is not just the cost associated with a potential exposure resulting in an illness or infection and not just the actual monetary cost, but the cost of non-compliance. This really gets at monitoring program progress over time. This can be via a "Secret Shopper" program with boots on the ground monitoring things like PPE use and compliance, donning and doffing compliance, and use of engineering controls like safer medical devices.

Cost in this sense may include the monetary penalties that may be involved in non-compliance from a Federal Agency like OSHA, EPA, DOT, or FDA. It could mean the cost of forfeiting accreditation from the Joint Commission. It could mean deductions in reimbursement from CMS. It could mean legal ramifications. It might also mean losing valuable staff or patient load. Cost comes in many forms if a program is not designed, run, and evaluated well.

Improving Compliance

Facilities all over the world struggle with compliance with infectious disease controls. In the United States alone, compliance with a process like donning PPE prior to entering a room with transmission or contact precautions can range as low as 7% to up to 22% for a pathogen of concern as important as *Clostridium difficile* (Yanke et al. 2015).

Clinical researchers from Michigan identified three ways compliance with precaution practices (protecting both patient and personnel from exposure) happens (Krein et al. 2018):

1. Violations: Deviations from safe operating practices or procedures
2. Process or procedural mistakes: Failures of intention
3. Slips: Failures of execution

Non-compliance can result in self-, patient, or environmental contamination and potential exposures. Violations may involve entering a room with a patient on isolation precautions with clear signage, without donning appropriate PPE (e.g., gown). Mistakes may involve improper PPE removal or pulling a stethoscope from around the neck to over the gown and back again. Slips include touching one's face or computer screen or smart phone with contaminated gloves.

Putting a program in place to assess compliance with precautions can be a great way to improve processes and relationships across different disciplines including employee/occupational health, infection prevention, operating room (OR), risk management, materials management, environmental safety, and patient advocates. All would agree that improving precaution compliance means improving safety and quality across the healthcare and public health spectrum.

Mistakes may happen as urgent cases can result in loss of focus on all but the patient or because training needs to be reinforced (wrong sequence of donning and doffing). Mistakes are generally a result of faulty planning or underestimating perceptions of time. Slips can result from distractions or failing to think through processes prior to implementation. Violations, however, must not be happening and may be a result of the culture and climate of safety in the facility and/or breakdown of institutional controls (Chap. 8).

You, alone, are not to blame if the overall culture or climate of safety within your institution is failing, but you are responsible to communicate challenges, strains, opportunities, and resolutions upward to management and leadership and most of all to the community of co-workers, colleagues, and personnel that you serve in your role.

References

Krein, S. L., Mayer, J., Harrod, M., et al. (2018). Identification and characterization of failures in infectious agent transmission precaution practices in hospitals: A quantitative study. *JAMA Internal Medicine, 178*(8), 1016–1022. https://doi.org/10.1001/jamainternmed.2018.1898.

Yanke, E., Zellmer, C., Van Hoof, S., Moriarty, H., Carayon, P., & Safdar, N. (2015). Understanding the current state of infection prevention to prevent *Clostridium difficile* infection: A human factors and systems engineering approach. *American Journal of Infection Control, 43*(3), 241–247. https://doi.org/10.1016/j.ajic.2014.11.026.

Appendix A: OSHA Forms for Recording Work-Related Injuries and Illnesses

© Springer Nature Switzerland AG 2020
A. H. Mitchell, *Preventing Occupational Exposures to Infectious Disease in Health Care*, https://doi.org/10.1007/978-3-030-56039-3

OSHA's Form 300 (Rev. 01/2004)

Log of Work-Related Injuries and Illnesses

Year 20____

U.S. Department of Labor
Occupational Safety and Health Administration

Form approved OMB no. 1218-0176

Attention: This form contains information relating to employee health and must be used in a manner that protects the confidentiality of employees to the extent possible while the information is being used for occupational safety and health purposes.

You must record information about every work-related death and about every work-related injury or illness that involves loss of consciousness, restricted work activity or job transfer, days away from work, or medical treatment beyond first aid. You must also record significant work-related injuries and illnesses that are diagnosed by a physician or licensed health care professional. You must also record work-related injuries and illnesses that meet any of the specific recording criteria listed in 29 CFR Part 1904.8 through 1904.12. Feel free to use two lines for a single case if you need to. You must complete an Injury and Illness Incident Report (OSHA Form 301) or equivalent form for each injury or illness recorded on this form. If you're not sure whether a case is recordable, call your local OSHA office for help.

Establishment name _____

City _____ State _____

Identify the person

(A) Case no.

(B) Employee's name

(C) Job title (e.g., Welder)

Describe the case

(D) Date of injury or onset of illness — month/day

(E) Where the event occurred (e.g., Loading dock north end)

(F) Describe injury or illness, parts of body affected, and object/substance that directly injured or made person ill (e.g., Second degree burns on right forearm from acetylene torch)

Classify the case

CHECK ONLY ONE box for each case based on the most serious outcome for that case:

(G) Death
(H) Days away from work

Remained at Work
(I) Job transfer or restriction
(J) Other recordable cases

Enter the number of days the injured or ill worker was:

(K) Away from work — ___ days
(L) On job transfer or restriction — ___ days

Check the "Injury" column or choose one type of illness:

(M)
(1) Injury
(2) Skin disorder
(3) Respiratory condition
(4) Poisoning
(5) Hearing loss
(6) All other illnesses

Page totals

Be sure to transfer these totals to the Summary page (Form 300A) before you post it.

Page ___ of ___

Public reporting burden for this collection of information is estimated to average 14 minutes per response, including time to review the instructions, search and gather the data needed, and complete and review the collection of information. Persons are not required to respond to the collection of information unless it displays a currently valid OMB control number. If you have any comments about these estimates or any other aspects of this data collection, contact: US Department of Labor, OSHA Office of Statistical Analysis, Room N-3644, 200 Constitution Avenue, NW, Washington, DC 20210. Do not send the completed forms to this office.

Appendix B: Model Exposure Control Plan

NOTE: This plan is adapted from the OSHA Enforcement Procedures for the Occupational Exposure to Bloodborne Pathogens Compliance Directive (CPL 02-02-069 Appendix D) to have broader application to not only bloodborne but other infectious diseases as well.

The Model Exposure Control Plan is intended to serve employers as an example exposure control plan which is required by the Bloodborne Pathogens Standard. A central component of the requirements of the standard is the development of an exposure control plan (ECP).

The intent of this model is to provide small employers with an easy-to-use format for developing a written exposure control plan. Each employer will need to adjust or adapt the model for their specific use.

The information contained in this publication is not considered a substitute for the OSH Act or any provisions of OSHA standards. It provides the general guidance on a particular standard-related topic but should not be considered a definitive interpretation for compliance with OSHA requirements. The reader should consult the OSHA standard in its entirety for specific compliance requirements.

Policy

___(Facility Name)___ is committed to providing a safe and healthful work environment for our entire staff. In pursuit of this endeavor, the following expose control plan (ECP) is provided to eliminate or minimize occupational exposure to infectious disease.

The ECP is a key document to assist our firm in implementing and ensuring compliance with the standard, thereby protecting our employees. This ECP includes:

- Determination of employee exposure
- Implementation of various methods of exposure control, including:

© Springer Nature Switzerland AG 2020
A. H. Mitchell, *Preventing Occupational Exposures to Infectious Disease in Health Care*, https://doi.org/10.1007/978-3-030-56039-3

Universal precautions
Engineering and work practice controls
Personal protective equipment
Housekeeping

- Hepatitis B vaccination or any other vaccination required for job duties
- Post-exposure evaluation and follow-up
- Communication of hazards to employees and training
- Recordkeeping
- Procedures for evaluating circumstances surrounding an exposure incident

The methods of implementation of these elements of the standard are discussed in the subsequent pages of this ECP.

Program Administration

In blank spaces below, enter name of responsible person or department for each element.

_____is (are) responsible for the implementation of the ECP. _____will maintain, review, and update the ECP at least annually and whenever necessary to include new or modified tasks and procedures.

Contact location/phone number: _____

- Those employees who are determined to have occupational exposure to blood or other potentially infectious materials (OPIM) and/or infectious diseases must comply with the procedures and work practices outlined in this ECP.
- _____ will maintain and provide all necessary personal protective equipment (PPE), engineering controls (e.g., sharps injury prevention devices, sharps containers), labels, and red bags as required by the standard.
- _____ will ensure that adequate supplies of the aforementioned equipment are available in the appropriate sizes.
- Contact location/phone number: _____
- _____ will be responsible for ensuring that all medical actions required are performed and that appropriate employee health and OSHA records are maintained. Contact location/phone number:

  _____

- _____ will be responsible for training, documentation of training, and making the written ECP available to employees, OSHA, and NIOSH representatives.

Contact location/phone number: _____

Employee Exposure Determination

The following is a list of all jobs and classifications at our establishment in which **ALL** employees have occupational exposure:

JOB TITLE	DEPARTMENT/LOCATION
(Example: Nurse)	*(ICU)*

The following is a list of job classifications in which **SOME** employees at our establishment have occupational exposure. Included is a list of tasks and procedures, or groups of closely related tasks and procedures, in which occupational exposure may occur for these individuals:

JOB TITLE	DEPARTMENT/LOCATION	TASK/PROCEDURE
(Example: EVS Tech	*Environmental Services*	*Handling Regulated Waste)*

Part-time, temporary, contract, and per diem *employees are covered by the standard. How the provisions of the standard will be met for these employees should be described in the ECP.*

Methods of Implementation and Control

All employees will utilize standard precautions for infection prevention and control.

Exposure Control Plan

Employees receive an explanation of this ECP during their initial training session. It will also be reviewed in their annual refresher training. All employees have an opportunity to review this plan at any time during their work shifts by contacting _____. If requested, we will provide an employee with a copy of the ECP free of charge and within 15 days of the request.

_____ is responsible for reviewing and updating the ECP annually or more frequently if necessary to reflect a new or modified task or procedure that affects occupational exposure and to reflect new or revised employee positions with occupational exposure.

Engineering Controls and Work Practices

Engineering controls and work practice controls will be used to prevent or minimize exposure to bloodborne pathogens. The specific engineering controls and work practice controls used are listed below:

- _(For example: non-glass tubes, blunt tip suture needles, needleless systems)_
- _____
- _____

Sharps disposal containers are inspected and maintained or replaced by _____ every _____ *(list frequency)* _____ or whenever necessary to prevent overfilling.

This facility identifies the need for changes in engineering control and work practices through *(Examples: Review of OSHA records, employee interviews, committee activities,* etc.*)* _____

We evaluate new procedure or new products regularly by

(Describe the process, literature reviews, supplier info, products considered)

_____
_____
_____

Both frontline workers and management officials are involved in this process: *(Describe how employees will be involved)*

_____
_____

_____ will ensure effective implementation of these recommendations.

Personal Protective Equipment (PPE)

PPE is provided to our employees at no cost to them. Training is provided by _____ in the use of the appropriate PPE for the tasks or procedures employees will perform.

The types of PPE available to employees are as follows for each department/unit/ procedure where they are needed *(Ex., respirators, gloves, eye protection,* etc.*)* ____

_____
_____

PPE is located in all _____ *(List locations)* _____.

If additional PPE is needed, it may be obtained through_____

(Specify how employees are to obtain PPE and who is responsible for ensuring that it is available.)

All employees using PPE must observe the following precautions:

- Wash hands with soap and running water immediately or as soon as feasible after removal of gloves or other PPE. If sinks are not available, hand-rubs can be used, but hands must be washed as soon as possible after that.
- Remove PPE after it becomes contaminated, and before leaving the work area.
- Used PPE may be disposed of in _____

(List appropriate containers for storage, laundering, decontamination, or disposal.)

- Wear appropriate gloves when it can be reasonably anticipated that there may be hand contact with blood or OPIM, known or suspected infected or ill patients, and patient specimens, and when handling or touching contaminated items are surfaces; replace gloves if torn, punctured, or contaminated, or if their ability to function as a barrier is compromised.
- Utility gloves may be decontaminated for reuse if their integrity is not compromised; discard utility gloves if they show signs of cracking, peeling, tearing, puncturing, or deterioration.
- Never wash or decontaminate disposable gloves, gowns, or respirators for reuse.
- Wear appropriate face and eye protection when splashes, sprays, spatters, or droplets of blood or OPIM pose a hazard to the eyes, nose, or mouth.
- Remove immediately or as soon as feasible any garment contaminated by blood or OPIM, in such a way as to avoid contact with the outer surface.

The procedure for handling used PPE is as follows:
(For example, how and where to decontaminate face shields, eye protection, resuscitation equipment. May refer to specific agency procedure by title or number and last date of review)

_____
_____
_____

Environmental Services

Regulated and/or infectious waste is placed in containers which are closeable, constructed to contain all contents and prevent leakage, appropriately labeled or color-coded (see Labels), and closed prior to removal to prevent spillage or protrusion of contents during handling.

The procedure for handling **sharps disposal containers** is: *(may refer to specific agency procedure by title or number and last date of review)*

_____
_____
_____

The procedure for handling **other regulated or infectious waste** (red bags, etc.) is: *(may refer to specific agency procedure by title or number and last date of review)*

_____

_____

_____

Contaminated sharps are discarded immediately or as soon as possible in containers that are closeable, puncture-resistant, leakproof on sides and bottoms, and labeled or color-coded appropriately. Sharps disposal containers must be easily accessible and as close as feasible to the immediate area where sharps are used and are available at this location in each room and/or area where they are needed_____

Basins and pails (e.g., wash or emesis basins) are cleaned and decontaminated as soon as feasible after visible contamination.

Broken glassware which may be contaminated is picked up using mechanical means, such as a brush and dustpan.

Laundry

The following contaminated articles will be laundered by this facility:

_____

_____

Laundering will be performed by _____ at *(time and/or location)*   .
The following laundering requirements must be met:

- Handle contaminated laundry as little as possible, with minimal agitation.
- Place laundry from known or suspected sick/ill people using this protocol

_____.

- Place wet contaminated laundry in leakproof, labeled or color-coded containers before transport. Use red bags with biohazard symbols for this purpose.
- Wear the following PPE when handling and/or sorting contaminated laundry:

_____.

Labels

The following labeling method(s) is used in this facility:

EQUIPMENT TO BE LABELED   LABEL TYPE (size, color, etc.)
(e.g., specimens, contaminated laundry, etc.)   *(red bag, biohazard label,* etc.)

_____   _____

_____   _____

_____ will ensure warning labels are affixed or red bags are used as required if regulated wasted or contaminated equipment is brought into the facility. Employees are to notify _____ if they discover regulated waste containers, refrigerators containing blood or OPIM, contaminated equipment, etc. without proper labels.

Hepatitis B Vaccination

_____ will provide training to employees on hepatitis B vaccinations, addressing the safety, benefits, efficacy, methods of administration, and availability.

The hepatitis B vaccination is available at no cost after training and within 10 days of initial assignment to employees identified in the exposure determination section of this plan. Vaccination is encouraged unless (1) documentation exists that the employee has previously received the series, (2) antibody testing reveals that the employee is immune, or (3) medical evaluation shows that vaccination is contraindicated.

However, if an employee chooses to decline vaccination, the employee must sign a declination form. Employees who decline may request and obtain the vaccination as later date at no cost. Documentation of refusal of the vaccination is kept at _____ *by* _____.
Vaccination   will   be   provided   by   _____   at _____.

Following the medical evaluation, a copy of the healthcare professional's written opinion will be obtained and provided to the employee. It will be limited to whether the employee requires the hepatitis vaccine and whether the vaccine was administered.

Exposure Evaluation and Follow-Up

Should an exposure incident occur, contact _____
at the following number: _____.
An immediately available confidential medical evaluation and follow-up will be conducted by _____.
Following the initial first aid (clean the wound, flush eyes or other mucous membrane, etc.), the following activities will be performed:

- Document the routes of exposure and how the exposure occurred.
- Identify and document the source individual (unless the employer can establish that identification is infeasible or prohibited by state or local law).

- Obtain consent and plan to have the source individual tested as soon as possible to determine HIV, HCV, and HBV infectivity; document that the source individual's test results were conveyed to the employee's healthcare provider.
- If the source individual is already known to be HIV, HCV, and/or HBV positive, new testing need not to be performed.
- Assure that the exposed employee is provided with the source individual's test results and with information about applicable disclosure laws and regulations concerning the identity and infectious status of the source individual (e.g., laws protecting confidentiality).
- After obtaining consent, collect exposed employee's blood as soon as feasible after exposure incident, and test blood for HBV and HIV serological status.
- If the employee does not give consent for HIV serological testing during collection of blood for baseline testing, preserve the baseline blood sample for at least 90 days; if the exposed employee elects to have the baseline sample tested during this waiting period, perform testing as soon as feasible.

Administration of Post-exposure Evaluation and Follow-Up

_____ ensures that healthcare professional(s) responsible for employee's hepatitis B vaccination and post-exposure evaluation and follow-up are given a copy of OSHA's Bloodborne Pathogens Standard.

_____ ensures that the healthcare professional evaluating an employee after an exposure incident receives the following:

- A description of the employee's job duties relevant to the exposure incident
- Route(s) of exposure
- Circumstances of exposure
- If possible, results of the source individual's blood test
- Relevant employee medical records, including vaccination status

_____ provides the employee with a copy of the evaluating healthcare professional's written opinion within 15 days after completion of the evaluation.

Procedures for Evaluating the Circumstances Surrounding an Exposure Incident

_____ will review the circumstances of all exposure incidents to determine:

- Engineering controls in use at the time
- Work practices followed

- A description of the device being used (including type and brand)
- PPE used at the time of the exposure incident (*gloves, eye shields,* etc.)
- Location of the incident (*O.R., E.R., patient room,* etc.)
- Procedures being performed when the incident occurred
- Employee's training

_____ will record all percutaneous injuries from contaminated sharps in the Sharps Injury Log.

If it is determined that revisions need to be made, _____ will ensure that appropriate changes are made to this ECP. (*Changes may include an evaluation of safer devices, adding employees to the exposure determination list,* etc.)

Employee Training

All employees who have occupational exposure to bloodborne and/or infectious pathogens receive training conducted by _____ _____. (*Attach a brief description of their qualifications.*)

All employees who have occupational exposure to bloodborne pathogens receive training on the epidemiology, symptoms, and transmission of bloodborne pathogen diseases. In addition, the training program covers, at minimum, the following elements:

- A copy and explanation of the standard
- An explanation of our ECP and how to obtain a copy
- An explanation of methods to recognize tasks and other activities that may involve exposure to blood and OPIM and/or infectious disease, including what constitutes an exposure incident
- An explanation of the use and limitations of engineering controls, work practices, and PPE
- An explanation of the types, uses, location, removal, handling, decontamination, and disposal of PPE
- An explanation of the basis for PPE selection
- Information on the hepatitis B vaccine, including information on its efficacy, safety, methods of administration, the benefits of being vaccinated, and that the vaccine will be offered free of charge
- Information on the appropriate actions to take and persons to contact in an emergency involving blood or OPIM
- An explanation of the procedure to follow if an exposure incident occurs, including the method of reporting the incident and the medical follow-up that will be made available
- Information on the post-exposure evaluation and follow-up that the employer is required to provide for the employee following an exposure incident

- An explanation of the sings and labels and/or color coding required by the standard and used at this facility
- An opportunity for interactive questions and answers with the person conducting the training session

Training materials for this facility are available at _____.

Recordkeeping

Training Records

Training records are completed for each employee upon completion of training. These documents will be kept for at least **3 years** at _____.
  The training records include:

- The dates of the training sessions
- The contents or a summary of the training sessions
- The names and qualifications of persons conducting the training
- The names and job titles of all persons attending the training sessions

  Employee training records are provided upon request to the employee of the employee's authorized representative within 15 working days. Such request should be addressed to

_____.

Medical Records

Medical records are maintained for each employee with occupational exposure in accordance with 29 CFR 1910.1020, "Access to Employee Exposure and Medical Records."
_____ is responsible for maintenance of the required medical records. These **confidential** records are kept at _____ for at least the **duration of employment plus 30 years.**
  Employee medical records are provided upon request of the employee or to anyone having written consent of the employee with 15 working days. Such request should be sent to _____.

OSHA Recordkeeping

An exposure incident is evaluated to determine if the case meets OSHA's Recordkeeping Requirements (29 CFR 1904). This determination and the recording activities are done by

_____.

Sharps Injury Log

In addition to the 1904 Recordkeeping Requirements, all percutaneous injuries from contaminated sharps are also recorded in the Sharps Injury Log. All incidences must include at least:

- The date of the injury
- The type and brand of the device involved
- The department or work are where the incident occurred
- An explanation of how the incident occurred.

This log is reviewed at least annually as part of the annual evaluation of the program and is maintained for at least 5 years following the end of the calendar year that they cover.

If a copy is requested by anyone, it must have any personal identifiers removed from the report.

Establishment/Facility Name: _____

Douglas County

Department Name:_____

Sharps Injury Log					Year 200_____
Date	Case/ report no.	Type of device (e.g., syringe, suture needle)	Brand name of device	Work area where injury occurred [e.g., geriatrics, lab]	Brief description of how the incident occurred [i.e., procedure being done, action being performed (disposal, injections, etc.), body party injured]

29 CFR 1910.1030, OSHA's Bloodborne Pathogens Standard, in paragraph (h)(5), requires an employer to establish and maintain a Sharps Injury Log for recording all percutaneous injuries in a facility occurring from *contaminated* sharps. The purpose of the Log is to aid in the evaluation of devices being used in health care and other facilities and to identify problem devices or procedures requiring addition attention or review. This log must be kept in addition to the injury and illness log required by 29 CFR 1910. The Sharps Injury Log should include all sharps injuries occurring in a calendar year. The log must be retained for 5 years following the end of the year to which it relates. The log must be kept in a manner that preserves the confidentiality of the affected employee.

Hepatitis B Vaccine Declination (Mandatory)

I understand that due to my occupational exposure to blood or other potentially infectious materials, I may be at risk of acquiring hepatitis B virus (HBV) infection. I have been given the opportunity to be vaccinated with hepatitis B vaccine, at no charge to myself. However, I decline hepatitis B vaccination at this time. I understand that by declining this vaccine, I continue to be at risk of acquiring hepatitis B, a serious disease. If in the future I continue to have occupational exposure to blood or other potentially infectious materials and I want to be vaccinated with hepatitis B vaccine, I can receive the vaccination series at no charge to me.

Employee signature: _____

Date: _____

Appendix C: Hazard Communication Safety Data Sheet

The following table provides the minimum information needed to communicate important information related to occupational exposure to hazardous chemicals (OSHA 2012).

These can be found in detail on OSHA's website: https://www.osha.gov/laws-regs/regulations/standardnumber/1910/1910.1200AppD

Heading	Subheading
1. Identification	(a) Product identifier used on the label; (b) Other means of identification; (c) Recommended use of the chemical and restrictions on use; (d) Name, address, and telephone number of the chemical manufacturer, importer, or other responsible party; (e) Emergency phone number.
2. Hazard(s) identification	(a) Classification of the chemical in accordance with paragraph (d) of §1910.1200;(b) Signal word, hazard statement(s), symbol(s) and precautionary statement(s) in accordance with paragraph (f) of §1910.1200. (Hazard symbols may be provided as graphical reproductions in black and white or the name of the symbol, e.g., flame, skull and crossbones); (c) Describe any hazards not otherwise classified that have been identified during the classification process;(d) Where an ingredient with unknown acute toxicity is used in a mixture at a concentration $\geq 1\%$ and the mixture is not classified based on testing of the mixture as a whole, a statement that X% of the mixture consists of ingredient(s) of unknown acute toxicity is required.

Heading	Subheading
3. Composition/ information on ingredients	Except as provided for in paragraph (i) of §1910.1200 on trade secrets:
	For Substances
	(a) Chemical name;
	(b) Common name and synonyms;
	(c) CAS number and other unique identifiers;
	(d) Impurities and stabilizing additives which are themselves classified and which contribute to the classification of the substance.
	For Mixtures
	In addition to the information required for substances:
	(a) The chemical name and concentration (exact percentage) or concentration ranges of all ingredients which are classified as health hazards in accordance with paragraph (d) of §1910.1200 and
	(1) Are present above their cut-off/concentration limits; or
	(2) Present a health risk below the cut-off/concentration limits.
	(b) The concentration (exact percentage) shall be specified unless a trade secret claim is made in accordance with paragraph (i) of §1910.1200, when there is batch-to-batch variability in the production of a mixture, or for a group of substantially similar mixtures (See A.0.5.1.2) with similar chemical composition. In these cases, concentration ranges may be used.
	For All Chemicals Where a Trade Secret is Claimed
	Where a trade secret is claimed in accordance with paragraph (i) of §1910.1200, a statement that the specific chemical identity and/or exact percentage (concentration) of composition has been withheld as a trade secret is required.
4. First-aid measures	(a) Description of necessary measures, subdivided according to the different routes of exposure, i.e., inhalation, skin and eye contact, and ingestion; (b) Most important symptoms/effects, acute and delayed. (c) Indication of immediate medical attention and special treatment needed, if necessary.
5. Fire-fighting measures	(a) Suitable (and unsuitable) extinguishing media. (b) Specific hazards arising from the chemical (e.g., nature of any hazardous combustion products). (c) Special protective equipment and precautions for fire-fighters.
6. Accidental release measures	(a) Personal precautions, protective equipment, and emergency procedures. (b) Methods and materials for containment and cleaning up.
7. Handling and storage	(a) Precautions for safe handling. (b) Conditions for safe storage, including any incompatibilities.
8. Exposure controls/ personal protection	(a) OSHA permissible exposure limit (PEL), American Conference of Governmental Industrial Hygienists (ACGIH) Threshold Limit Value (TLV), and any other exposure limit used or recommended by the chemical manufacturer, importer, or employer preparing the safety data sheet, where available. (b) Appropriate engineering controls. (c) Individual protection measures, such as personal protective equipment.

Heading	Subheading
9. Physical and chemical properties	(a) Appearance (physical state, color, etc.);
	(b) Odor;
	(c) Odor threshold;
	(d) pH;
	(e) Melting point/freezing point;
	(f) Initial boiling point and boiling range;
	(g) Flash point;
	(h) Evaporation rate;
	(i) Flammability (solid, gas);
	(j) Upper/lower flammability or explosive limits;
	(k) Vapor pressure;
	(l) Vapor density;
	(m) Relative density;
	(n) Solubility(ies);
	(o) Partition coefficient: n-octanol/water;
	(p) Auto-ignition temperature;
	(q) Decomposition temperature;
	(r) Viscosity.
10. Stability and reactivity	(a) Reactivity;
	(b) Chemical stability;
	(c) Possibility of hazardous reactions;
	(d) Conditions to avoid (e.g., static discharge, shock, or vibration);
	(e) Incompatible materials;
	(f) Hazardous decomposition products.
11. Toxicological information	Description of the various toxicological (health) effects and the available data used to identify those effects, including:
	(a) Information on the likely routes of exposure (inhalation, ingestion, skin and eye contact);
	(b) Symptoms related to the physical, chemical and toxicological characteristics;
	(c) Delayed and immediate effects and also chronic effects from short- and long-term exposure;
	(d) Numerical measures of toxicity (such as acute toxicity estimates).
	(e) Whether the hazardous chemical is listed in the National Toxicology Program (NTP) Report on Carcinogens (latest edition) or has been found to be a potential carcinogen in the International Agency for Research on Cancer (IARC) Monographs (latest edition), or by OSHA.
12. Ecological information (Non-mandatory)	(a) Ecotoxicity (aquatic and terrestrial, where available);
	(b) Persistence and degradability;
	(c) Bioaccumulative potential;
	(d) Mobility in soil;
	(e) Other adverse effects (such as hazardous to the ozone layer).
13. Disposal considerations (Non-mandatory)	Description of waste residues and information on their safe handling and methods of disposal, including the disposal of any contaminated packaging.

Heading	Subheading
14. Transport information (Non-mandatory)	(a) UN number;
	(b) UN proper shipping name;
	(c) Transport hazard class(es);
	(d) Packing group, if applicable;
	(e) Environmental hazards (e.g., Marine pollutant (Yes/No));
	(f) Transport in bulk (according to Annex II of MARPOL 73/78 and the IBC Code);
	(g) Special precautions which a user needs to be aware of, or needs to comply with, in connection with transport or conveyance either within or outside their premises.
15. Regulatory information (Non-mandatory)	Safety, health and environmental regulations specific for the product in question.
16. Other information, including date of preparation or last revision	The date of preparation of the SDS or the last change to it.

[77 FR 17884, March 26, 2012] https://www.osha.gov/laws-regs/regulations/standardnumber/191 0/1910.1200AppD

Index

© Springer Nature Switzerland AG 2020
A. H. Mitchell, *Preventing Occupational Exposures to Infectious Disease in Health Care*, https://doi.org/10.1007/978-3-030-56039-3

Printed in the United States
by Baker & Taylor Publisher Services